# An Aging Population

*Opposing Viewpoints*®

# AN AGING POPULATION

*Opposing Viewpoints*®

# Other Books of Related Interest

# AN AGING POPULATION

*Opposing Viewpoints*®

Laura K. Egendorf, *Book Editor*

Daniel Leone, *Publisher*
Bonnie Szumski, *Editorial Director*
Scott Barbour, *Managing Editor*

OPPOSING
VIEWPOINTS®
SERIES

Greenhaven Press, Inc., San Diego, California

Cover photo: Photodisc

Library of Congress Cataloging-in-Publication Data

An aging population / Laura Egendorf, book editor.
    p.  cm. — (Opposing viewpoints series)
    Includes bibliographical references and index.
    ISBN 0-7377-0781-X (pbk. : alk. paper) —
ISBN 0-7377-0782-8 (lib. : alk. paper)
    1. Aged—United States. 2. Aging—United States.
3. Gerontology—United States. I. Egendorf, Laura K., 1973–
II. Series.

HQ1064.U5 A6353  2002
305.26'0973—dc21
                                                          2001023051
                                                          CIP

Greenhaven Press, Inc., P.O. Box 289009
San Diego, CA 92198-9009

"Congress shall make
no law. . .abridging the
freedom of speech, or of
the press."

*First Amendment to the U.S. Constitution*

The basic foundation of our democracy is the First
Amendment guarantee of freedom of expression.
The Opposing Viewpoints Series is dedicated to the
concept of this basic freedom and the idea that it is
more important to practice it than to enshrine it.

# Contents

# Why Consider Opposing Viewpoints?

*"The only way in which a human being can make some approach to knowing the whole of a subject is by hearing what can be said about it by persons of every variety of opinion and studying all modes in which it can be looked at by every character of mind. No wise man ever acquired his wisdom in any mode but this."*

John Stuart Mill

In our media-intensive culture it is not difficult to find differing opinions. Thousands of newspapers and magazines and dozens of radio and television talk shows resound with differing points of view. The difficulty lies in deciding which opinion to agree with and which "experts" seem the most credible. The more inundated we become with differing opinions and claims, the more essential it is to hone critical reading and thinking skills to evaluate these ideas. Opposing Viewpoints books address this problem directly by presenting stimulating debates that can be used to enhance and teach these skills. The varied opinions contained in each book examine many different aspects of a single issue. While examining these conveniently edited opposing views, readers can develop critical thinking skills such as the ability to compare and contrast authors' credibility, facts, argumentation styles, use of persuasive techniques, and other stylistic tools. In short, the Opposing Viewpoints Series is an ideal way to attain the higher-level thinking and reading skills so essential in a culture of diverse and contradictory opinions.

In addition to providing a tool for critical thinking, Opposing Viewpoints books challenge readers to question their own strongly held opinions and assumptions. Most people form their opinions on the basis of upbringing, peer pressure, and personal, cultural, or professional bias. By reading carefully balanced opposing views, readers must directly confront new ideas as well as the opinions of those with whom they disagree. This is not to simplistically argue that everyone who reads opposing views will—or should—change his or her opinion. Instead, the series enhances readers' understanding of their own views by encouraging confrontation with opposing ideas. Careful examination of others' views can lead to the readers' understanding of the logical inconsistencies in their own opinions, perspective on why they hold an opinion, and the consideration of the possibility that their opinion requires further evaluation.

## Evaluating Other Opinions

To ensure that this type of examination occurs, Opposing Viewpoints books present all types of opinions. Prominent spokespeople on different sides of each issue as well as well-known professionals from many disciplines challenge the reader. An additional goal of the series is to provide a forum for other, less known, or even unpopular viewpoints. The opinion of an ordinary person who has had to make the decision to cut off life support from a terminally ill relative, for example, may be just as valuable and provide just as much insight as a medical ethicist's professional opinion. The editors have two additional purposes in including these less known views. One, the editors encourage readers to respect others' opinions—even when not enhanced by professional credibility. It is only by reading or listening to and objectively evaluating others' ideas that one can determine whether they are worthy of consideration. Two, the inclusion of such viewpoints encourages the important critical thinking skill of objectively evaluating an author's credentials and bias. This evaluation will illuminate an author's reasons for taking a particular stance on an issue and will aid in readers' evaluation of the author's ideas.

It is our hope that these books will give readers a deeper understanding of the issues debated and an appreciation of the complexity of even seemingly simple issues when good and honest people disagree. This awareness is particularly important in a democratic society such as ours in which people enter into public debate to determine the common good. Those with whom one disagrees should not be regarded as enemies but rather as people whose views deserve careful examination and may shed light on one's own.

Thomas Jefferson once said that "difference of opinion leads to inquiry, and inquiry to truth." Jefferson, a broadly educated man, argued that "if a nation expects to be ignorant and free . . . it expects what never was and never will be." As individuals and as a nation, it is imperative that we consider the opinions of others and examine them with skill and discernment. The Opposing Viewpoints Series is intended to help readers achieve this goal.

David L. Bender and Bruno Leone,
Founders

---

Greenhaven Press anthologies primarily consist of previously published material taken from a variety of sources, including periodicals, books, scholarly journals, newspapers, government documents, and position papers from private and public organizations. These original sources are often edited for length and to ensure their accessibility for a young adult audience. The anthology editors also change the original titles of these works in order to clearly present the main thesis of each viewpoint and to explicitly indicate the opinion presented in the viewpoint. These alterations are made in consideration of both the reading and comprehension levels of a young adult audience. Every effort is made to ensure that Greenhaven Press accurately reflects the original intent of the authors included in this anthology.

# Introduction

*"Ageism is a social phenomenon . . . most entrenched in industrial and post-industrial civilizations such as the United States."*

— *sociologists Ursula A. Falk and Gerhard Falk*

Older Americans are faced with a variety of stereotypes. They are seen by many people as being feeble in mind and body and as economic burdens on society, and they are labeled with pejoratives such as "geezers" or "old fogies." Even though the average American has a lifespan of 76.5 years—and those who reach the age of sixty-five can expect to live another eighteen years—it is often believed that they have little to contribute once they reach their sixties. However, this stereotype exists not just in the United States, but in other nations as well.

At one time, American attitudes toward the elderly were more positive. In the seventeenth and eighteenth centuries, the aging were respected and venerated because they helped transmit wisdom and tradition to the younger generations. They were given the best seats in church, and Puritan teachings instructed youth on how to behave toward their elders. One reason that the aged garnered this respect was because there were so few of them in colonial society. According to social historian David Hackett Fischer, only two percent of the population at that time was over sixty-five years old.

By the nineteenth century, American society had changed significantly. Ironically, the elderly suffered as America progressed. The rise of an urban and industrialized nation meant that the skills and education of many of the aged were no longer useful. Because younger, healthier workers were more desirable for factories, mandatory retirement laws were passed as early as 1777. These laws forced the aging to leave their jobs, leading to poverty. Old-age homes were established for those elderly who were poor and had no family to look after them; such homes further isolated the elderly from society. No longer were the aged referred to in respectful terms, as labels such as "codger" and "fuddy-duddy" began to take hold in the nineteenth century.

The negative attitudes toward the elderly have continued into the twentieth and twenty-first centuries. Many aged persons are isolated from their families; the majority live alone or with their spouse, with 60 percent of women over the age of eighty-five living alone. Commercials and jokes frequently rely on stereotypes of the elderly, such as the belief that they are desperate to appear young and virile. Some people believe the Social Security system allows senior citizens to drain money away from tax-paying workers. However, for the aging Americans who do want to continue to work or return to the workplace, age discrimination often raises a barrier. In their book *Ageism, the Aged and Aging in America*, Ursula A. Falk and Gerhard Falk describe the plight of the elderly who are healthy and want to find work but are made irrelevant because of their age: "Since occupation and work are the principal criteria of social prestige in America, the old, by being excluded from work are therefore devalued."

The United States is not unique in its attitudes toward the elderly. In other cultures and nations, the rise of urban industrialization has led to similar results. In African and Asian nations, when those countries were largely rural, older relatives used to live with their children and grandchildren. However, the limited space of urban housing makes such intergenerational homes less practical and less desirable. As a consequence, the elderly in these countries have lost their status in the family and society as a whole. Nana Araba Apt, a professor of sociology at the University of Ghana at Legon, writes that the increasing urbanization of African life has worsened the status of the elderly. In the past, the elderly were heavily involved in the rearing of children, helped make important decisions for the family, and were supported as they aged. As society became more urban, the aged began to lose their economic security. Furthermore, Apt writes, "They lost their former favored position in the extended family. No longer were the grandfather and grandmother the center of absorbing social life of their descendants but often became unwanted hangers on . . . in the activities of their children and grandchildren." Japanese society has changed in a similar fashion.

Although 55 percent of elderly parents live with their children and grandchildren—nearly three times the rate in other industrialized nations—that percentage has dropped sharply since 1970, when 80 percent of homes housed multiple generations. According to Nicholas D. Kristof, a writer for the *New York Times*, this is an example of how "Japanese attitudes are changing very rapidly and . . . many young Japanese feel even less of a debt to their parents than do young Americans."

Despite the devalued status of the elderly in many cultures, aging is not a universally negative experience. In their book *Successful Aging*, John W. Rowe and Robert L. Kahn refute many of the stereotypes associated with the aging process, such as the beliefs that the elderly are in poor health or unable to learn new skills. Rowe and Kahn also note that many elderly Americans contribute significantly to society and the economy but that since much of the work done by the elderly is unpaid, it does not receive its rightful recognition. They write: "Almost all older men and women are productive in this larger sense. One-third work for pay and one-third work as volunteers in churches, hospitals, and other organizations."

The attitudes toward the aging in America have long been evolving. In *Aging Population: Opposing Viewpoints*, the status of and attitudes toward the elderly are examined in the following chapters: How Does Society View Aging and the Elderly? How Will an Aging Population Affect America? Should Social Security Be Reformed? Are Improvements Needed in Elderly Health Care? In those chapters, the authors consider how the aging are treated in America and what steps should be taken, if necessary, to improve that treatment.

# CHAPTER 1

# How Does Society View Aging and the Elderly?

# Chapter Preface

In the sixteenth century, Spanish explorer Ponce de León sought the "fountain of youth," a source of water that could restore youth. While no such fountain has ever been found, many people—cognizant that aging is often associated with weakness and poor health—have tried to stymie the aging process.

There are several approaches to slowing down the aging process. Thirty thousand Americans take shots of estrogen, testosterone, or the human growth hormone, which strengthens the immune system and increases bone mass and muscle. Other options include exercise, eating healthier foods, reducing alcohol and tobacco use, and cosmetic surgery. Toby Mayer, the medical codirector of the Beverly Hills Institute of Aesthetic and Reconstructive Surgery, asserts that baby boomers have valid reasons for elective plastic surgery. According to Mayer, such surgery lets older Americans age gracefully and "has entered the mainstream as an increasingly popular option that helps maintain a high standard and quality of life."

These efforts to create a modern fountain of youth have met with concern and criticism. The *American Medical News* notes that some doctors are worried about the widespread use of the human growth hormone because it can increase the risk of breast, prostate, and colon cancers. Others criticize the very notion of slowing down the aging process. In an opinion piece for the *New York Times*, Melvin Maddocks, a man in his seventies, writes: "[The] boomers shouldn't count on converting us to their credo on modern immaturity, based as it is on the simplistic assumption that being young is the same as being happy." Clara Silverstein, writing for *Boomer* magazine, suggests that middle-age Americans need to be more self-accepting and not turn to surgery as a way to feel better about themselves.

The quest for eternal youth may never end. While it might be possible to slow down the aging process, the act of aging—and consequently the ways in which people respond to it—cannot be avoided. In the following chapter, the authors evaluate the ways in which society views aging and the elderly.

❖

*"We younger, healthier people sometimes avoid the old to avoid our own fears of aging."*

# Society Fears the Aging Process

Mary Pipher

Americans fear the processes of aging and dying, Mary Pipher contends in the following viewpoint. She claims that younger and healthier adults often avoid spending time around the aging because they want to avoid the issues of mortality and loss of independence. In addition, she contends that negative views of the aging process are portrayed in the media and expressed through the use of pejorative words to describe the elderly. Pipher is a psychologist and author of several books, including *Another Country: Navigating the Emotional Terrain of Our Elders*, the book from which this viewpoint was excerpted.

As you read, consider the following questions:

1. According to Pipher, what are the two types of birthday cards that relate to aging?
2. Why does the author think *retirement* is an ugly word?
3. What is America's highest virtue, in Pipher's opinion?

From *Another Country*, by Mary Pipher. Copyright © 1999 by Mary Pipher. Used by permission of Riverhead Books, a division of Penguin Putnam, Inc.

We segregate the old for many reasons—prejudice, ignorance, a lack of good alternatives, and a youth-worshiping culture without guidelines on how to care for the old. The old are different from us, and that makes us nervous. Xenophobia means fear of people from another country. In America we are xenophobic toward our old people.

## How Greeting Cards Reflect Culture

An anthropologist could learn about us by examining our greeting cards. As with all aspects of popular culture, greeting cards both mirror and shape our realities. Cards reflect what we feel about people in different roles, and they also teach us what to feel. I visited my favorite local drugstore and took a look.

There are really two sets of cards that relate to aging. One is the grandparent/grandchild set that is all about connection. Even a very dim-witted anthropologist would sense the love and respect that exist between these two generations in our culture. Young children's cards to their grandparents say, "I wish I could hop on your lap," or, "You're so much fun." Grandparents' cards to children are filled with pride and love.

There is another section of cards on birthdays. These compare human aging to wine aging, or point out compensations. "With age comes wisdom, of course that doesn't make up for what you lose." We joke the most about that which makes us anxious. "Have you picked out your bench at the mall yet?" There are jokes about hearing loss, incontinence, and losing sexual abilities and interest. There are cards on saggy behinds, gray hair, and wrinkles, and cards about preferring chocolate or sleep to sex. "You know you're getting old when someone asks if you're getting enough and you think about sleep."

## Fears of Aging and Dying

Poking fun at aging isn't all bad. It's better to laugh than to cry, especially at what cannot be prevented. However, these jokes reflect our fears about aging in a youth-oriented culture. We younger, healthier people sometimes avoid the old to avoid our own fears of aging. If we aren't around dying people, we don't have to think about dying.

We baby boomers have been a futureless generation, raised in the eternal present of TV and advertising. We have allowed ourselves to be persuaded by ads that teach that if we take good care of ourselves, we will stay healthy. Sick people, hospitals, and funerals destroy our illusions of invulnerability. They force us to think of the future.

Carolyn Heilbrun said, "It is only past the meridian of fifty that one can believe that the universal sentence of death applies to oneself." Before that time, if we are healthy, we are likely to be in deep denial about death, to feel as if we have plenty of time, that we have an endless vista ahead. But in hospitals and at funerals, we remember that we all will die in the last act. And we don't necessarily appreciate being reminded.

## A Youth-Oriented Society

In the United States, the normative expectation is that people will be active, achievement oriented, productive, and able to plan for the future. Aged persons generally do not meet these expectations because these are norms for young adults. The United States is a youth-oriented society, a situation that can easily be verified by examining the range of consumer goods and advertising that emphasizes youthfulness—even for elderly people. For example, cosmetic companies in the 1990s are grappling with how to approach the increasingly larger population of older consumers. The trend has been to emphasize the youthful looks and beauty that an older woman can maintain if she fights against looking old by using cosmetics.

Regardless, to be old is to enter a stage of life that is socially devalued, because it indicates that the person no longer participates in adult roles on the same level as before. . . . This problem is compounded by the lessened physical appeal assigned to the old by a youth-oriented society.

William C. Cockerham, *This Aging Society*, 1997.

When I first visited rest homes, I had to force myself to stay. What made me most upset was the thought of myself in a place like that. I didn't want to go there, literally or figuratively. Recently I sat in an eye doctor's office surrounded by old people with white canes. Being in this room gave me intimations of mortality. I thought of Bob Dylan's line: "It's not dark yet, but it's getting there."

We know the old-old will die soon. The more we care and the more involved we are with the old, the more pain we feel at their suffering. Death is easier to bear in the abstract, far away and clinical. It's much harder to watch someone we love fade before our eyes. It's hard to visit an uncle in a rest home and realize he no longer knows who we are or even who he is. It's hard to see a grandmother in pain or drugged up on morphine. Sometimes it's so hard that we stay away from the people who need us the most.

Our culture reinforces our individual fears. To call something old is to insult, as in *old hat* or *old ideas*. To call something young is to compliment, as in *young thinking* or *young acting*. It's considered rude even to ask an old person's age. When we meet an adult we haven't seen in a long time, we compliment her by saying, "You haven't aged at all." The taboos against acknowledging age tell us that aging is shameful.

Many of the people I interviewed were uncomfortable talking about age and were unhappy to be labeled old. They said, "I don't feel old." What they meant was, "I don't act and feel like the person who the stereotypes suggest I am." Also, they were trying to avoid being put in a socially undesirable class. In this country, it is unpleasant to be called old, just as it is unpleasant to be called fat or poor. The old naturally try to avoid being identified with an unappreciated group. . . .

## The Elderly Are Treated Poorly

Nothing in our culture guides us in a positive way toward the old. Our media, music, and advertising industries all glorify the young. Stereotypes suggest that older people keep younger people from fun, work, and excitement. They take time (valuable time) and patience (in very short supply in the 1990s). We are very body-oriented, and old bodies fail. We are appearance-oriented, and youthful attractiveness fades. We are not taught that old spirits often shimmer with beauty.

Language is a problem. Old people are referred to in pejorative terms, such as *biddy, codger,* or *geezer,* or with cutesy words, such as *oldster, chronologically challenged,* or *senior citizen.* People describe themselves as "eighty years young." Even *retirement* is an ugly word that implies passivity, uselessness, and withdrawal from the social and working world. Many of the old are offended by ageist stereotypes and jokes. Some internalize these beliefs and feel badly about themselves. They stay with their own kind in order to avoid the harsh appraisals of the young.

Some people do not have good manners with the old. I've seen the elderly bossed around, treated like children or simpletons, and simply ignored. Once in a cafe, I heard a woman order her mother to take a pill and saw the mother wince in embarrassment. My mother-in-law says she sees young people but they don't see her. Her age makes her invisible.

In our culture the old are held to an odd standard. They are admired for not being a bother, for being chronically cheerful. They are expected to be interested in others, bland in their opinions, optimistic, and emotionally generous. But the young certainly don't hold themselves to these standards.

Accidents that old drivers have are blamed on age. After a ninety-year-old friend had his first car accident, he was terrified that he would lose his license. "If I were young, this accident would be perceived as just one of those things," he pointed out. "But because I am old, it will be attributed to my age." Now, of course, some old people are bad drivers. But so are some young people. To say "He did that because he's old" is often as narrow as to say, "He did that because he's black" or "Japanese." Young people burn countertops with hot pans, forget appointments, and write overdrafts on their checking accounts. But when the old do these same things, they experience double jeopardy. Their mistakes are not viewed as accidents but rather as loss of functioning. Such mistakes have implications for their freedom.

## Media Stereotypes

As in so many other areas, the media hurts rather than helps with our social misunderstandings. George Gerbner reported on the curious absence of media images of people older than sixty-five. Every once in a while a romantic movie plot might involve an older man, but almost never an older woman. In general, the old have been cast as silly, stubborn, and eccentric. He also found that on children's programs, older women bear a disproportionate burden of negative characteristics. In our culture, the old get lumped together into a few stereotyped images: the sweet old lady, the lecherous old man, or the irascible but soft-hearted grandfather. Almost no ads and billboards feature the old. Every now and then an ad will show a grandparent figure, but then the grandparent is invariably youthful and healthy.

In *Fountain of Age*, Betty Friedan noted that the old are portrayed as sexless, demented, incontinent, toothless, and childish. Old women are portrayed as sentimental, naive, and silly gossips, and as troublemakers. A common movie plot is the portrayal of the old trying to be young—showing them on motorbikes, talking hip or dirty, or liking rock and roll. Of course there are exceptions, such as *Nobody's Fool, On Golden Pond, Mr. and Mrs. Bridge, Driving Miss Daisy, Mrs. Brown*, and *Twilight*. But we need more movies in which old people are portrayed in all their diversity and complexity.

The media is only part of much larger cultural problems. We aren't organized to accommodate this developmental stage. For example, being old-old costs a lot of money. Assisted-living housing, medical care, and all the other services the old need are expensive. And yet, most old people can't earn money. It's true that some of our elders are wealthy, but many live on small incomes. Visiting the old, I heard tragic stories involving money. I met Arlene, who, while dying of cancer, had to fear losing her house because of high property taxes. I met Shirley, who lived on noodles and white rice so that she could buy food for her cat and small gifts for her grandchildren. I met people who had to choose between pills and food or heat.

## The American Obsession with Independence

Another thing that makes old age a difficult stage to navigate is our American belief that adults need no one. We think of independence as the ideal state for adults. We associate independence with heroes and cultural icons such as the Marlboro man and the Virginia Slims woman, and we associate dependence with toxic families, enmeshment, and weakness. To our postmodern, educated ears, a psychologically healthy but dependent adult sounds oxymoronic.

We all learn when we are very young to make our own

personal declarations of independence. In our culture, *adult* means "self-sufficient." Autonomy is our highest virtue. We want relationships that have no strings attached instead of understanding, as one lady told me, "Honey, life ain't nothing but strings."

These American ideas about independence hurt families with teens. Just when children most need guidance from parents, they turn away from them and toward peers and media. They are socialized to believe that to be an adult, they must break away from parents. Our ideas about independence also hurt families with aging relatives. As people move from the young-old stage into the old-old stage, they need more help. Yet in our culture we provide almost no graceful ways for adults to ask for help. We make it almost impossible to be dependent yet dignified, respected, and in control.

As people age, they may need help with everything from their finances to their driving. They may need help getting out of bed, feeding themselves, and bathing. Many would rather pay strangers, do without help, or even die than be dependent on those they love. They don't want to be a burden, the greatest of American crimes. The old-old often feel ashamed of what is a natural stage of the life cycle. In fact, the greatest challenge for many elders is learning to accept vulnerability and to ask for help.

If we view life as a time line, we realize that all of us are sometimes more and sometimes less dependent on others. At certain stages we are caretakers, and at other stages we are cared for. Neither stage is superior to the other. Neither implies pathology or weakness. Both are just the results of life having seasons and circumstances. In fact, good mental health is not a matter of being dependent or independent, but of being able to accept the stage one is in with grace and dignity. It's an awareness of being, over the course of one's lifetime, continually interdependent.

## Rethinking Dependency

In our culture the old fear their deaths will go badly, slowly, and painfully, and will cost lots of money. Nobody wants to die alone, yet nobody wants to put their families through too much stress. Families are uneasy as they negotiate this rocky terrain. The trick for the younger members is to help without feeling trapped and overwhelmed. The trick for older members is to accept help while preserving dignity and control. Caregivers can say, "You have nurtured us, why wouldn't we want to nurture you?" The old must learn to say, "I am grateful for your help and I am still a person worthy of respect."

As our times and circumstances change, we need new language. We need the elderly to become elders. We need a word for the neediness of the old-old, a word with less negative connotations than *dependency*, a word that connotes wisdom, connection, and dignity. *Dependency* could become mutuality or *interdependency*. We can say to the old: "You need us now, but we needed you and we will need our children. We need each other."

However, the issues are much larger than simply which words to use or social skills to employ. We need to completely rethink our ideas about caring for the elderly. Like the Lakota, we need to see it as an honor and an opportunity to learn. It is our chance to repay our parents for the love they gave us, and it is our last chance to become grown-ups. We help them to help ourselves.

We need to make the old understand that they can be helped without being infantilized, that the help comes from respect and gratitude rather than from pity or a sense of obligation. In our society of disposables and planned obsolescence, the old are phased out. Usually they fade away graciously. They want to be kind and strong, and, in America, they learn that to do so means they should ask little of others and not bother young people.

Perhaps we need to help them redefine kindness and courage. For the old, to be kind ought to mean welcoming younger relatives' help, and to be brave ought to mean accepting the dependency that old-old age will bring. We can reassure the old that by showing their children how to cope, they will teach them and their children how well this last stage can be managed. This information is not peripheral but rather something everyone will need to know.

*"Most older people enjoy the same level of
emotional well-being and life satisfaction as
younger adults."*

# Aging Can Be a Positive Experience

Paul B. Baltes and Margret M. Baltes

In the following viewpoint, Paul B. Baltes and Margret M.
Baltes argue that the aging experience is positive for many
older adults, although they caution that it is a more negative
experience for adults in their mid-eighties and beyond. The
authors maintain that people in their sixties and seventies
have the same level of emotional well-being as younger
adults. They also note that these older adults have a greater
capacity for wisdom and can help other people benefit from
what they have learned. However, the authors contend that
people who are in advanced old age experience significant
losses in their ability to function psychologically and mentally. Paul B. Baltes is the director of the Center for Lifespan
Psychology at the Berlin Max Planck Institute for Human
Development. Prior to her death in 1999, Margret M. Baltes
was a professor of psychological gerontology at the Free
University of Berlin.

As you read, consider the following questions:
1. According to the authors, people function well
   psychologically until what age?
2. How does the Berlin Max Planck Institute for Human
   Development define "wisdom," as noted by the Balteses?
3. According to the Balteses, what is advanced old age like
   psychologically?

The passions of humankind for aging well, and the associated scientific as well as societal activities, have spawned outcomes that signal progress. Although it is not yet clear whether the world as a whole does equally well, industrialized societies have demonstrated remarkable efficacy and flexibility in extending longevity for many people and in providing the economic and social resources for them to lead a more satisfying life in old age. Yes, there are unmet challenges and shortfalls, for instance, regarding health care, the stability of pension plans, old-age-friendly transportation, and the social opportunities for older people to create lives with a sense of purpose and productivity. Nevertheless, most experts agree that these challenges can be met if we approach them in a timely, targeted, and concerted way.

As behavioral scientists, we can also report positive findings in the mental, emotional, and personality domains of human functioning. At least up to age seventy-five or so, most people function well psychologically. Humans suffer some losses in intelligence and memory, but for most people these losses are relatively small and do not interfere with everyday functioning. Moreover, in terms of emotional well-being and life satisfaction, the news is surprisingly excellent.

Throughout our lives and perhaps especially in old age, we are continuously adjusting our standards of expectation. As a consequence, most older people enjoy the same level of emotional well-being and life satisfaction as younger adults.

## The Psychology of the Elderly

In a sense, psychology outwits reality, including biology. We human beings are outfitted with a remarkable psychological sense of self-protection and self-repair. Strategies of psychological resilience are among our best abilities. For instance, as older adults experience major illnesses with increased frequency, they compare themselves with others who have experienced similar or even worse illnesses. Moreover, we view others as worse off, thereby elevating our own standing in comparison.

In old age, this resilience is tested to its limits but continues to deliver the goods; that is, the ability to adjust and to transform reality so that the self continues to feel alive and flourish, continues to operate well if not better than in earlier years. Because of this remarkable power of the self, older adults on average are not at all more depressed or anxious than younger ones. On the contrary, as shown for instance in the Berlin Aging Study by Jacqui Smith, Alexandra Freund, Ursula Staudinger, and colleagues, people aged seventy to eighty continue to have a purpose in life, and for the most part they live in the present with much engagement, mastering the tasks of everyday life.

The good news of old age even includes some aspects of psychological functioning where there is hope for age-associated advance in functioning. Two examples are emotional intelligence and wisdom. In emotional intelligence, that is, the ability to understand the causes of emotions (such as hate, love, or anxiety) and the ways to control and use them effectively for problem solving, we seem to improve with age. This improvement is particularly noticeable when difficult and interpersonal problems of life are involved.

## Age Brings Wisdom

The second example of an instance of positive aging and a new frontier of mastery is wisdom. Historically, wisdom is the peak of human excellence, the perfect integration of knowledge and character. In research conducted by Paul Baltes and Ursula Staudinger at the Berlin Max Planck Institute for Human Development, wisdom is defined as "expert knowledge about life in general and good judgment and advice about how to conduct oneself in the face of complex, uncertain circumstances."

To test for wisdom, we present people in our laboratory with difficult hypothetical dilemmas. One might be: "Imagine that a fifteen-year-old girl tells you she is thinking about getting married right away. What might you think about and tell her to consider?" The responses we get to these and other dilemmas vary widely. A participant might respond: "A fifteen-year-old girl wants to get married? No way; marrying at age fifteen is utterly wrong." Another answer might reflect a deeper knowledge of the human condition: "Well, on the surface this seems easy. On average, marrying at age fifteen is not a good thing. On the other hand, many girls think about it when they fall in love for the first time without, however, getting married in the end. And then, there are situations where the average case doesn't fit; special life circumstances, you know: a terminal illness, or having just lost one's parents. Or the fifteen-year-old girl might not be from this country, but from one where earlier marriages are the rule. I would need to know more about the specific circumstances to say more."

The second reply demonstrates the kind of cultural and experiential knowledge about the human condition that one can accumulate over a lifetime and that the Berlin research group defines as wisdom:

• rich knowledge of the course, variations, and complexities of the human condition;

• recognition of the relativity of values and priorities within a set of cultural universals;

• a good sense of the uncertainties of life and the insight that any life decision involves a particular balance of gains and losses, especially if considered from the point of view of a lifetime; and finally

• the notion that wisdom reflects empathy and an interest in the well-being of oneself and others.

Our research results have supported the notion that wisdom is a domain where older adults can excel. The longer our research has gone on, the more we have come to think that someone in the third season of life, someone who is sixty or seventy years old, may well hold the "world record" in wisdom. In additional research, we also have shown that our store of wisdom benefits from the ability to engage ourselves with others in discussions of life dilemmas and from having a personality that is open to new experiences and strives toward excellence in matters of human lives. Older adults in particular seem to have acquired the dispositions and skills to benefit from such social exchanges with others to solve a dilemma of life. Here may lie the foundation for the many success stories of grandfathers, grandmothers, and older mentors who are able to express warmth, understanding, and guidance.

For us, such findings on the age-friendliness of wisdom-related knowledge and skills are cause for optimism. Only during the last century have so many people reached old age. With more and more people living longer, and thus—at least potentially—growing wiser and wiser, who is to say what the aging mind may contribute in the future?

## Insufficient Support Structures

There are other reasons why we believe that there is much as yet inactivated potential for aging well. On the sociocultural level, for instance, support structures for the optimization of old age are underdeveloped. There is a dearth of social roles, for instance, that society offers to older citizens.

Moreover, can the usual adult focus on economic productivity be transformed into other forms of productivity in old age—for instance, forms of productivity that highlight the self, the interpersonal, and the intergenerational?

To appreciate the underdevelopment of cultural support of old age, we need only compare our "culture of old age" with that for childhood, where over centuries we have worked toward refining a system of childhood education and outlining desirable goals of life and ways to attain these goals. Education for the golden years, however, is just in the making. Or consider, as another example of new ways to prepare for old age, our better understanding of the important role of health behavior (such as non-smoking and physical exercise) in the promotion of healthy aging, as well as the emerging power of biomedical genetic interventions to repair and prevent conditions of illness. As a consequence, today's seventy-year-olds are already healthier and more vital than their age peers of several decades ago. The continued improvement of the health status of same-age seventy- or eighty-year-olds over recent decades may be the trend of the future.

What we have summarized so far coalesces in the conclusion that human aging has come a long way and that old age has a future. The social-technological-scientific advances of the twentieth century and our individual psychological make-ups form a powerful coalition that can generate for most people a satisfying Third Age. With the Third Age we refer to a concept advanced by the British social historian Peter Laslett. It refers approximately to the age spectrum from sixty up to seventy-five years.

What about advanced old age, however, what we call the Fourth Age? More and more people live into their late eighties, nineties, and even hundreds. Evidence is increasing that the Fourth Age, the added years beyond age eighty-five or so, will not harbor the same potential as earlier gains in life expectancy, that the passion for aging well will face increasingly difficult obstacles as people move into the Fourth Age. The scientific evidence is both theoretical and empirical.

## Dramatic Changes in Longevity

Over the past hundred years a silent and unprecedented revolution in longevity has occurred: people living in the industrialized world have on average gained 25 years of life, thanks largely to reduction of deaths at childbirth and infancy, and to control of diseases associated with old age. This is nearly equal to life expectancy advances over the preceding 5,000 years. In many countries, the 85-plus age group is the most rapidly growing.

The next century may bring even more dramatic increases. Prevention and elimination of disease along with control over the aging process itself could push our life spans from a world average of 66 years today to closer to 110 or 120 years.

Robert Butler, *UNESCO Courier*, January 1999.

On a theoretical level, one of us (Paul Baltes) has outlined an overall architecture or evolutionary "building plan" of the life course and identified advanced old age as the most radical form of vulnerability or "incompleteness." Paul Baltes has argued that this architecture is less like the well-conceived incompleteness of an "unfinished Schubert symphony" than it is like a plan whose built-in weaknesses become conspicuous as old age is reached. Why is this so? Evolution—because of its primary focus on biological reproductive fitness during early adulthood—has not invested much work in the optimization of old age. Thus the genome-related foundation for healthy biological aging is weak and not a good friend of old age. As a consequence of this biological deficit, culture-based interventions, including processes of learning and social support, are also less efficient in old age. It takes more and more cultural, technological, and behavioral resources to attain and maintain high levels of functioning as people move into the ninth and tenth decades of their lives.

Such a pessimistic view of advanced old age finds support in recent empirical studies of the very old that alert us to increasing dysfunctionality in advanced old age. The Berlin Aging Study, because of its wide age range (seventy-to-one-hundred-year-olds), heterogeneous sampling, and broad interdisciplinary assessment, is one example. It offers a new window on the quality of life in advanced old age.

Contrary to findings on the "young old" or the Third Age, the negative consequences of aging become more general and glaring when people in their late eighties and nineties are studied. In advanced old age, practically *all* people show substantial losses in *all* domains of psychological functioning—for instance, in all domains of cognitive functioning. Similarly, average changes in personality functioning—though they continue to be smaller than those in intelligence and memory—point in the same direction during the Fourth Age, that is, toward more dysfunctionality. Furthermore, in advanced old age, more and more people express fewer positive emotions, including a sense of loneliness. Psychologically speaking, advanced old age increasingly becomes a kind of testing-the-limits situation for psychological resilience, with such overdemand and stress that previously effective strategies of adaptation and life management begin to fail.

The relatively pessimistic picture of the Fourth Age of aging, the late eighties and nineties, is perhaps most apparent and disconcerting when we consider the most prevalent mental illness that afflicts old people, that is, senile dementia of the Alzheimer's type. In the Berlin Aging Study—and its findings are consistent with work of others—researchers under the leadership of psychiatrist Hanfried Helinchen observed that the prevalence of all diagnoses (mild, moderate, severe) of Alzheimer's dementia increased from about 2 to 3 percent in seventy-to-eighty-year-olds, to 10 to 15 percent in eighty-to-ninety-year-olds, to about 50 percent in over-ninety-year-olds. Alzheimer's disease is the condition that older people fear most. Its manifestations are often outside the realm of dignity that humans aspire to for themselves. If the recent trend toward an increase in remaining lifetime for the oldest old continues, it is likely that the incidence of Alzheimer's disease will increase as well.

The Fourth Age, aging from about eighty onward, then, seems to present a new scenario. The oldest old are not simply people who continue to stay alive because their functional status remains at the same level as that of the younger old in the Third Age. In the Fourth Age, there seem to be much more severe constraints on what efforts at optimization can achieve. And, as we mentioned before, the reasons for this increased limitation are several, and they lie in the biological and cultural architecture of the life course. First, evolution neglected old age, and therefore biological potential and reserves wane with age. Second, for positive development to extend into later and later phases of the life span, more and more, cultural and technological compensation is required. Third, because of the age-linked weakening of biological potential, the efficiency of cultural factors and support systems decreases with age. This reduction in efficiency of cultural factors is the more worrisome because it is exactly those factors from which a more positive outcome can be expected.

It is in the nature of human evolution and the human spirit to believe that one solution to the dramatic challenge of the Fourth Age is cultural-technological-scientific progress. Indeed, we need to keep in mind that the future of old age is not something we simply enter; the future is also something we help create. However, it appears to us that the degree of biological incompleteness and vulnerability in advanced old age is a radical one and qualitatively different from that in the Third Age. Thus we will find it more and more difficult to make the interventions we will need to ensure, for most people in the Fourth Age, the kind of functional status in which gains outnumber losses and where human flourishing and dignity prevail. Designing an improved culture for the Fourth Age of life will be one of the principal challenges of the next century.

*"Four areas of economic age discrimination can generally be recognized."*

# Age Discrimination Toward Older Workers Is Prevalent

Ursula Adler Falk and Gerhard Falk

In the following viewpoint, Ursula Adler Falk and Gerhard Falk maintain that aging Americans face considerable economic discrimination, especially in the workplace. For example, the authors assert, older workers are sometimes fired regardless of their job performance or passed over for promotions in favor of younger employees. According to the Falks, older Americans suffer a loss of social honor and prestige as a result of this economic exclusion. Ursula Adler Falk, a psychotherapist and gerontologist, and Gerhard Falk, a sociologist and historian, are the co-authors of *Ageism, the Aged and Aging in America: On Being Old in an Alienated Society*, the book from which this viewpoint was excerpted.

As you read, consider the following questions:
1. How do political skills in the workplace affect how older workers are evaluated, in the authors' opinion?
2. What is the paradox concerning aging and productivity in contemporary America, according to the Falks?
3. According to the authors, what are the consequences of territorial age segregation?

Age discrimination is found in the private and the public sector of the economy. It is found at all levels of skill and education, and it is found at all levels of income and among both sexes.

## Different Types of Economic Discrimination

Four areas of economic age discrimination can generally be recognized. The first of these is preference given to youthful applicants in jobs which can also be performed by older workers. An example was the erstwhile practice of allowing only young women to perform the task of flight attendants. This has changed under pressure of the Age Discrimination in Employment Act (ADEA) as well as public opinion so that now men as well as older women serve lunch at 30,000 feet.

A second area of age discrimination in the economy was the practice of discharging employees at an older age regardless of job performance. These cases are hard to prove and difficult to litigate. This is mainly true because job performance can be a subjective criterion often influenced by both the self-fulfilling prophecy and office politics.

Third, economic ageism has been related to limiting promotion opportunities to younger employees. Personnel decisions based on age stereotyping are very common. Beliefs about aging and middle-aged personnel, are so entrenched that many an unspoken decision deprives older workers of well-deserved promotions solely because of the prejudice of a supervisor or manager. These decisions are generally made in the context of performance ratings by managers concerning supervisees. The evidence is that there is a negative age-performance rating relationship and that this relationship is mainly influenced by the type of performance measure used. This means that *when objective productivity indices were used, there was a pattern of increases in performance as age increased.* However, when supervisor ratings of performance were used, there was a tendency for ratings to be *lower* for older workers.

## Age-Based Prejudices

Therefore, it is reasonable to conclude that supervisors "see" the opposite of the facts. This is possible not only because performance ratings are so subjective, but also because prejudice leads to perceptions that are not well-intentioned in the first place.

Political skills are also responsible for the evaluations received by many employees. Those who know ingratiating tactics will be evaluated better than those who lack such skills. Since it has been found that older workers are less likely to use such tactics, it is possible that older workers often receive a lower evaluation than younger workers, not only because of the ageist prejudices already discussed, but also because of their failure to "kowtow" to supervisors who are often younger than they are.

This assault upon the economic and emotional stability of so-called "older" workers is therefore enhanced by the practice of permitting recent college graduates without any supervisory experience or with limited supervisory experience to become managers and thus supervise older employees.

By "older" is meant here anyone forty years old or older since the Age Discrimination in Employment Act defines age 40 as an age at which protection from age discrimination is mandated by that law.

> Virginia Stapleton is a fifty-nine-year-old woman who has been existing on welfare together with her invalid husband. She searched hard for a job in the secretarial field since she was an experienced typist for many years and has obtained skills in word processing. She searched the newspapers and answered a number of advertisements. When she did succeed in getting an interview she was treated with cold politeness. One potential employer was very blunt and without hesitation asked her, "What can you do for us at this stage of your life?" Even though Mrs. Stapleton wants the proverbial workfare, not welfare, she is unable to succeed.

[Wanda J.] Smith and [K. Vernard] Harrington have shown that age-based beliefs common in the United States at the end of the century are shared with the whole American population by young future managers. These beliefs include the view that older workers will not cooperate with younger supervisors and that the reverse is also true. Yet, such beliefs overlook that older workers have learned that failure to cooperate or show antagonism to a boss is career suicide.

Nevertheless, the relationship between a younger supervisor and an older worker does not fit the usual American norms. We define "norm" to mean anticipated behavior. Normally, then, individuals forty years old or more are viewed as authority figures, as leaders and as bosses. Teachers, clergy, parents and important elected officials are viewed as normally being older and experienced. Hence, the dyad younger boss-older worker is a role reversal in American culture and leads to tensions, resentments and anxiety.

## The Causes and Consequences of Age Exclusion

The fourth aspect of the old-young dyad in late century America is the practice of age exclusion. This phrase concerns all who place their aged parents in a nursing home, all who never visit their parents, all who persuade or even force their parents to give up their money before they are dead and a host of other such practices.

Age exclusion is the product of nonproductivity. This means that because of the increase in the life span and the increase of Americans who live long, many old Americans spend three decades in a post-productive stage. This age exclusion also affects the young who are segregated into schools. Hence, only the middle-aged are very productive in American life and, therefore they, the middle-aged, have almost all the power that is associated with a productive life.

Ever since the extended family has declined so that the generations live apart rather than together, the family has become a consumptive unit while in earlier years it was a productive unit which means that families were in business or in farming together.

Biologically, the old are actually more capable today than they were in earlier years and centuries. As longevity has increased, so has good health in old age increased. Hence, we are faced with the paradox that in [contemporary] America those who are more capable of leading a productive life are excluded from such productive activities because of the *social* definition of old age and not because those so excluded are physically old.

The consequences of exclusion are, of course, lack of power and lack of social prestige. Since occupation and work are the principal criteria of social prestige in America, the old, by being excluded from work are therefore devalued. Thus, the old suffer the same disadvantages and discrimination that other minorities suffer by reason of religion, or race or ethnic origin or gender. Three consequences of age discrimination are therefore identifiable. These are: economic discrimination, age stereotyping and territorial segregation.

"I see from your resume you used to be quite a bit younger. What made you change?"

Peter Steiner. Reprinted with permission.

Exclusion from employment has several consequences. One is, of course, reduction in social honor. Others are higher insurance premiums, difficulties in obtaining credit, and poverty. It is true that there are today more old Americans with good incomes than was true at any time in our past. It is also true, however, that old age poverty strikes particularly at those who do not have large pensions, insurance plans and, most of all, nursing home insurance. Since such insurance is extremely expensive while nursing homes require patients to pay upward of $50,000 per year, it is obvious that even those who saved and built considerable financial reserves over a lifetime can be impoverished in short order if faced with such costs.

Territorial age segregation has now become almost universal in the United States. For the young this refers to the huge college campus communities which exist in all states of the union. For the old, age segregation is found in the so-called Sun Belt communities which house only the old, such as Sun City, Arizona; Palm Springs, California and St. Petersburg, Florida. These and similar communities are age ghettos. The word ghetto is appropriate here since the first "ghetto" was the Jewish section of Venice which was so-named because the Hebrew word "get" means divorce or separation.

It is, of course, true that age ghettos exist because the old voluntarily move into such communities. Nevertheless, the consequences of such segregation are quite similar to the consequences of racial, ethnic or gender segregation. In particular this means that the old who live in such communities will only know other old people. Friendships between people of different age groups will hardly exist and behavior in such communities is rather uniform and rigid as there are no children and no young adults. Exclusion from the productive life of American society is the cause and the consequence of this segregation. This means that those who are already excluded by reason of age seek the comfort of living with others in the same situation and this segregation in turn increases the tendency to believe that all old people are incompetent, powerless and helpless. These beliefs are accepted by the old as well as the young who patronize, infantilize and reject the old. Thus, age exclusion deprives the American community of the experience the old have to offer and deprives the old of the vigor the younger generation commands. Tradition and continuity are also casualties of age segregation as is the interplay of the generations as children, grandchildren and grandparents know each other only as occasional visitors, voices on a telephone and abstractions sporadically visible and always at a distance.

The ever-increasing number of the old who live in retirement communities are the product of early retirement in a society in which longevity increases as well. Thus, more and more Americans spend a greater and greater number of years after their work life in the geronto-playpens labeled retirement communities.

*"Few of us would be comfortable if airline pilots or military officers could not be forced to retire at any age without proof of individual unfitness."*

# Age Discrimination Toward Older Workers Can Be Justified

Richard A. Posner

In the following viewpoint, Richard A. Posner asserts that employers often have valid reasons for discrimination toward employees on the basis of age. According to Posner, employers are not likely to be wrong about the skills of their employees because they have financial stakes in those evaluations. In addition, Posner contends that certain skills do decline with age and posits that mandatory retirement—such as requiring certain workers, like pilots, to retire at a certain age—has several advantages and is not discrimination. Posner is chief judge of the U.S. Court of Appeals for the Seventh Circuit and the author of a variety of books, including *Aging and Old Age*, from which this viewpoint is excerpted.

As you read, consider the following questions:

1. On what aspects of society does age discrimination law have a perverse impact, in the author's view?
2. What is "statistical discrimination," as defined by Posner?
3. In Posner's opinion, what are the financial advantages to retiring at the age of sixty-five?

E ven before the enactment of the Employee Retirement
 Income Security Act (ERISA) made it more likely that
an employer would resort to the threat of discharge (a threat
that to be credible would have to be carried out from time to
time) in order to discipline its employees, Congress had
made it more difficult to fire older employees by enacting
the Age Employment in Discrimination Act in 1967. The
Act, as subsequently amended, forbids employers to dis-
criminate on grounds of age against any employee aged 40
or over. Originally the protected class was 40 to 65, so
mandatory retirement at age 65 was permitted. The lid was
raised to 70 in 1978 and removed altogether in 1986.
Mandatory retirement at any age, along with any other measures retail or wholesale by which an employer treats an employee worse because of age, is, with a few exceptions, now
forbidden. I argue that the age discrimination law is largely
ineffectual but that to the extent it is effective it has a perverse impact both on the welfare of the elderly and on the
equality of income and wealth across the entire population.
The age discrimination law is at once inefficient, regressive,
and harmful to the elderly.

## The Causes of Age Discrimination

*Animus discrimination.* The justification offered for the law
was that people over 40 are subject to a form of prejudice,
"ageism," that is analogous to racism and sexism. After
putting to one side the use of the word as a synonym for anything that disadvantages an older worker (so presbyopia
would be "ageist"), we can posit two kinds of ageism, only
one plausible. The implausible is a systematic undervalua-
tion, motivated by ignorance, viciousness, or irrationality, of
the value of older people in the work place. This is sometimes referred to as "animus discrimination." I do not deny
that there is resentment and disdain of older people in our
society, or widespread misunderstandings, some disadvanta-
geous to the old. . . .
  But the [viewpoint] is about the work place. Even apart
from competitive pressures for rational behavior, which are
considerable in private markets, the people who make employment policies for corporate and other employers and

most of those who carry out those policies by making decisions about hiring or firing specific workers are at least 40 years old and often much older. It is as if the vast majority of persons who established employment policies and who made employment decisions were black, federal legislation mandated huge transfer payments from whites to blacks, and blacks occupied most high political offices in the nation. It would be mad in those circumstances to think the nation needed a law that would protect blacks from discrimination in employment. Employers—who have a direct financial stake in correctly evaluating the abilities of their employees and who for the most part are not young themselves—are unlikely to harbor either serious misconceptions about the vocational capacities of the old (so it is odd that employment should be the main area in which age discrimination is forbidden) or a generalized antipathy toward old people.

To put the point differently, the kind of "we-they" thinking that fosters racial, ethnic, and sexual discrimination is unlikely to play a large role in the treatment of the elderly worker. Not because a young person will (in all likelihood) someday be old; to put too much weight on the continuity of personal identity would slight the multiple-selves issue. But because the people who do the hiring and firing are generally as old as the people they hire and fire and are therefore unlikely to mistake those people's vocational abilities. One should not be surprised at how slight and equivocal the evidence that employers misconceive the ability of older workers is. Such workers do have trouble finding new jobs at high wages. But this is because the wages in their old jobs will have reflected firm-specific human capital that disappeared when they left and that they cannot readily replace because of the cost of learning new skills, and also because the proximity of these workers to (voluntary) retirement reduces the expected return from investing in learning new skills.

[A study by David Shapiro and Steven H. Sandell] found that "nearly 90 percent of [elderly] job losers' wage reductions are explained by the nontransferability of the workers' firm-specific skills and knowledge or seniority." The authors ascribed the remaining 10 percent to age discrimination, but they had no basis for this ascription. The 10 percent, as they acknowledged, was merely "a residual remaining after accounting for other factors"—and among the factors not accounted for was a possible age-related decline in capability. As the study was of the wages in new jobs of elderly workers who had lost their previous jobs, the possibility that the workers sampled were underperformers was indeed a significant one. The very next essay in the collection, a study of young and old workers employed by the same firm, finds that the *entire* difference in wages between the two groups is due to differences in investment in human capital. . . . Empirical findings that workers 65 or older perform their jobs as well as younger workers in the same enterprise are vitiated by selection bias: demonstrably unsatisfactory older workers will have been fired or nudged into retirement. The fact that *some* elderly people are able to perform to an employer's satisfaction is consistent with many not being able, in which event we would expect the average wages of elderly workers to be lower for reasons unrelated to discrimination.

One might think that if substandard elderly workers are weeded out, the average wages of the elderly employed would be no lower than those of the nonelderly employed, unless there were discrimination. But some of those weeded out of their current employment because they no longer perform to their employers' satisfaction will not leave the labor force; instead they will find lower-paying jobs, commensurate with their diminished capabilities, and their wages will depress the average.

The very idea of "animus" age discrimination rests on its own misconceptions—for example that employers insisted on mandatory retirement at fixed ages because they underestimated the capabilities of older people. As we shall see, that was not the reason.

## A More Plausible Form of Ageism

*Statistical discrimination.* The form of ageism (if it should be called that) that is more plausible and better substantiated than animus discrimination against the old consists of attributing to all people of a particular age the characteristics of the average person of that age. It is an example of what economists call statistical discrimination and noneconomists "stereotyping": the failure or refusal, normally motivated by the costs of information, to distinguish a particular member of a group from the average member. Age, like sex, is one of the first facts that we notice about a person and use to "place" him or her. We do this because we operate with a strong, though often an unconscious, presumption, echoing the rigid age grading that structures activities and occupations in many primitive societies, that particular attitudes, behaviors, and positions in life go with particular ages. "We judge one another with a notion of what status goes with what age: he's old to be a student, young to be a professor, old to marry, young to retire. Some people sometimes are 'off time' but most people most of the time 'act their age.'"

The presumption that age matters in these ways is rational. Otherwise this [viewpoint] would have no subject; any talk of "65-year-olds" or "octogenarians" would be as irrelevant to public policy as talk about the attitudes and behaviors of people with green eyes or chestnut hair. But there is a great deal of variance in the capacities, behaviors, and attitudes of persons in particular age groups and, partly as a result, great overlap between the capacities of persons in different age groups. People age at different rates and from different levels of capacity. So if age is used as a proxy for attributes desired or disliked by an employer, some people who are entirely competent to perform to the employer's specifications will not be hired, or will be fired or forced to retire to make way for young people who actually are less able.

This phenomenon does not, however, make age discrimination in employment inefficient any more than the substitution in some other field of activity of a rule (for example, do not drive faster than 65 miles per hour) for a standard (do not drive too fast for conditions) need be inefficient. A rule is simpler to administer than a standard and therefore cheaper, and the cost savings may exceed the loss from disregarding circumstances that may make the rule disserve the purposes behind it in a particular case. Rules have higher error costs but lower administrative costs, standards lower error costs but higher administrative costs, and the relative size of the two types of cost will determine the efficient choice between the alternative methods of regulation in particular settings.

Statistical discrimination is an example of rule-based behavior, and since it is a method of economizing on information costs we can expect it to be more common in settings where those costs are high. One is not surprised therefore that age grading (like literalism, another example of rule-based behavior designed to economize on information costs) is more common in primitive than in advanced societies. Yet even in advanced societies rules are frequently more efficient than standards; so mandatory retirement, and other employment classifications based on age, cannot be condemned out of hand as archaic. Few of us would be comfortable if airline pilots or military officers could not be forced to retire at any age without proof of individual unfitness.

## Age Affects Intelligence

Age discrimination is often quite rational. Employers have solid economic reasons for not wanting to hire and train employees who will soon be retiring. . . . Furthermore, people really do "slip" with age. . . . It is true that not all mental abilities are affected to the same extent, and not all individuals slip at the same rate. An exhaustive study of age-based slippage, published in 1998 in an issue of the journal *Intelligence*, showed that highly educated people with superior verbal skills retain those skills fairly well. Slippage is substantially greater in mathematical and spatial reasoning than in verbal reasoning. Nevertheless, all reasoning skills decline with age, and the decrement is greatest in what psychologists call "fluid intelligence," i.e., the ability to learn new tasks and see things in new ways. The ancient adage about old dogs and new tricks really has something to it.

Dan Seligman, *Forbes*, December 13, 1999.

Age grading illustrates how statistical discrimination can sometimes operate in favor of, rather than against, a particular group, here by ascription of the maturity, wisdom, and disinterest possessed by some old people to all or most of them. Another circumstance that has favored the old is that few people understand selection bias. People generalize from the impressive performance of octogenarian judges that octogenarians have unsuspected capabilities; but the advanced age at which most judges are appointed operates to draw judges from an unrepresentative segment of the aging population. If the elderly benefit from statistical discrimination as well as being hurt by it, maybe they would enjoy an undue advantage over other groups if the law succeeded in eradicating statistical discrimination against, as distinct from statistical discrimination in favor of, the elderly. I would not put too much weight on this factor, however. For reasons stated earlier, I would expect *employers* to have a generally clear-headed notion of the characteristics of the average worker in the different age groups and not be fooled by selection bias.

## The Advantages of Mandatory Retirement

Mandatory retirement—a blanket rule against retaining a worker who has reached a specified age, regardless of the particular worker's actual productivity—has three supports besides the general benefits of a rule. First, knowing far in advance the age at which one will retire facilitates an individual's financial and retirement planning. A person could always *decide* he was going to retire at some particular age, yet he might fear that he might change his mind—the multiple-selves problem, once again.

Second, because full social security benefits are available at age 65 and are sharply reduced until 70 if the recipient continues working after reaching 65, there are powerful financial advantages to retiring at 65. If, therefore, few workers would want to continue working after that point, the benefits from individualized assessment of their fitness to do so will be small, yet there are apt to be significant fixed costs of establishing and operating the requisite machinery of assessment. This point suggests that the abolition of mandatory retirement is unlikely to have a big effect on the labor-force participation of the elderly. . . .

Third, if, as is plausible, a significant decline in a worker's performance is probable within a few years after he reaches 65, the benefits from individualized assessment will be reduced further because they will be realized for only a short period. The costs of such assessment will rise, moreover, because the employer will have to monitor the performance of workers who have reached the stage of life at which a decline in job performance is highly probable more carefully than the performance of younger workers.

Conceivably the reaction against mandatory retirement, and the concern with age discrimination generally, may reflect the fact that statistical discrimination, being a function of information costs, probably is negatively correlated with education and IQ, since educated and intelligent people can absorb and use information more easily than other people. The "rigid" or "authoritarian" personality that psychologists associate with discriminatory attitudes can be given an economic meaning: people of lower intelligence or less education employ cruder screening devices, such as stereotyping. As information costs fall on average in a society, statistical discrimination increasingly becomes the domain of the uneducated and the unintelligent, so class prejudice may incline the society's elite to disparage or even forbid the practice.

I wonder how apt this point is to age discrimination in employment, though. The difference between an employee and an independent contractor has a bearing on this question. The difference is this: the employee does not sell his output to his principal, as the independent contractor does, but instead is paid for his time. Usually this is because the worker's output is difficult to value precisely, which may be because it is team output rather than individual output. The difficulty of valuation implies that assessment of the employee's contribution to the firm will be probabilistic rather than certain. The employer will be trying to infer that contribution from characteristics of the worker and of his performance. One characteristic is the worker's age. We know that age is often correlated with performance; and with age being directly observable and performance not, it may be entirely rational for even the most intelligent employer to use the former as a proxy for the latter.

# Periodical Bibliography

The following articles have been selected to supplement the diverse views presented in this chapter. Addresses are provided for periodicals not indexed in the *Readers' Guide to Periodical Literature*, the *Alternative Press Index*, the *Social Sciences Index*, or the *Index to Legal Periodicals and Books*.

W. Andrew Achenbaum
"Perceptions of Aging in America," *National Forum*, Spring 1998. Available from the Honor Society of Phi Kappa Phi, Box 16000, Louisiana State University, Baton Rouge, LA 70893.

*America*
"Keep an Eye on the Third Age," May 16, 1998.

Robert Butler
"The Longevity Revolution," *UNESCO Courier*, January 1999.

*Issues and Controversies on File*
"Age Discrimination," May 21, 1999. Available from Facts on File News Services, 11 Penn Plaza, New York, NY 10001-2006.

Margot Jefferys
"A New Way of Seeing Old Age Is Needed,"*World Health*, September/October 1996.

Ann Monroe
"Getting Rid of the Gray: Will Age Discrimination Be the Downfall of Downsizing?" *Mother Jones*, July/August 1996.

Bernadette Puijalon and Jacqueline Trincaz
"Sage or Spoilsport?" *UNESCO Courier*, January 1999.

Jody Robinson
"The Baby Boomers' Final Revolt," *Wall Street Journal*, July 31, 1998.

Dan Seligman
"The Case for Age Discrimination," *Forbes*, December 13, 1999.

Ruth Simon
"Too Damn Old," *Money*, July 1996.

John C. Weicher
"Life in a Gray America," *American Outlook*, Fall 1998. Available from 5395 Emerson Way, Indianapolis, IN 46226.

Ron Winslow
"The Age of Man," *Wall Street Journal*, October 18, 1999.

# CHAPTER 2

# How Will an Aging Population Affect America?

# Chapter Preface

As people age and leave the workplace, their income often decreases. While many among the elderly are financially secure, others are impoverished and need assistance. As the number of elderly in America grows, the issue of elderly poverty might seriously affect the nation.

Many people assert that American society needs to address the issue of elderly poverty, especially that of older women and minorities. In an article for the *American Prospect*, David Callahan, a fellow for the Century Foundation cites Census Bureau statistics showing that in 1997, 3.3 million Americans age sixty-five and older, or 10.5 percent of the aging population, lived below the poverty line. Approximately three-quarters of the elderly poor are women, and African-Americans comprise 24 percent of impoverished senior citizens. Women are disproportionately poor because the average annual income for an elderly woman in 1997 was $14,320, compared to $25,669 for elderly men. Although poverty among the elderly has been more than halved since 1967, Callahan asserts that such poverty should shame America. He offers suggestions for reducing the problem of elderly poverty, from increasing Social Security benefits to expanding housing programs.

However, other commentators assert that the average senior citizen is financially secure and does not need assistance from the government. Andrew Sullivan, a senior editor for the magazine *New Republic*, contends that the aging are not especially impoverished. He notes that the median net worth of senior citizens, according to the Census Bureau, is $86,000, "some 15 times the net worth of those under 35." Sullivan argues the elderly also have a significant amount of discretionary income, which enables them to travel extensively and enjoy quality medical care. He argues that this financial security should signal the end of the "culture of dependency" for wealthy senior citizens who have benefited from Social Security and other government programs.

The growing elderly population in America will likely have a significant economic and social impact. In the following chapter, the authors debate the ways in which an aging population will affect American society.

*"Global aging poses . . . fundamental economic challenges."*

# The Aging Population Is Hurting the Economy

Peter G. Peterson

In the following viewpoint, Peter G. Peterson argues that as the elderly population grows throughout the developed world, the global economy will suffer serious consequences. According to Peterson, benefit programs to the elderly will require increased funding, and taxes will need to be raised to provide those funds. He asserts that unless alternative solutions are implemented, these tax increases will wreck the standard of living for younger generations. Peterson was the secretary of commerce for President Richard Nixon and is the author of several books, including *Gray Dawn: How the Coming Age Wave Will Transform America—and the World.*

As you read, consider the following questions:

1. What percentage of the developed world will be elderly by 2030, according to Peterson?
2. According to Peterson, what will happen if the private savings rate falls by more than half over the next three decades?
3. What are the author's suggestions for meeting the needs of the elderly without overburdening the economy?

Reprinted, with permission, from Peter G. Peterson, "The Graying of the Developed Economies," *IntellectualCapital.com*, September 9, 1999, found at www.intellectualcapital.com/issues/issue289/item6326.asp.

An age wave of immense proportions is about to sweep over America and the rest of the developed world. For nearly all of history, the elderly never amounted to more than 2% or 3% of the population. With the industrial revolution, the share started to rise. Today in the developed world, the elderly amount to 14%. By 2030, they will reach 25%—and in some countries, they may be closing in on 30%.

This phenomenon, combined with the equally unprecedented decline in birth rates and the number of youth, defines the demographic parameters of global aging.

## Global Aging Will Change Society

Global aging promises to usher in a social transformation—even a revolution—with few parallels in humanity's past. It will subject the developed countries and their economies to enormous stresses, reshaping the family, redefining politics and cultures, and even rearranging the geopolitical order.

The benefit programs in the developed countries for the elderly are largely pay-as-you-go systems or, more bluntly, hand-to-mouth financing, and they have generated huge unfunded liabilities of about $70 trillion. That is, those benefits already are "earned" by today's workers for which nothing has been saved.

Over the next quarter-century, the number of retirees (beneficiaries) in the Organization for Economic Cooperation and Development (OECD) countries is projected to grow 14 times faster than the number of workers (taxpayers). And the ratio of taxpaying workers to non-working pensioners in the developed world is due to fall to 1.5-to-1—and in a few European countries it will drop to 1-to-1 or even lower.

## A Growing Economic Burden

As it does, the economic and fiscal burden of pay-as-you-go retirement systems will soar. All told, the cost of public benefits to the elderly is on track to grow by between 9% and 16% of gross domestic product in most of the developed countries.

This vast increase would be three to five times what the United States now spends on national defense. It also would represent an extra, and unthinkable, 25% to 40% taken out of every worker's taxable wages—in countries where total payroll tax rates often exceed 40% already. The time will come when the developed countries must confront the truth: that their universal pay-as-you-go retirement systems cannot sustain the coming age wave, and that their generosity must be greatly reduced. Will they change course in time to avoid massive deficits, massive and sudden draconian cuts in benefits, or massive tax hikes that wreck their economies, along with the living-standard prospects of younger generations?

The answer to the daunting question of how and when the social contract will be renegotiated will depend in part on how tomorrow's elderly use their growing political clout. By 2030, nearly half of all adults in developed countries and perhaps two-thirds of all voters will be at or beyond today's eligibility age for publicly subsidized retirement benefits.

Beyond the fiscal and social burden, global aging poses even more fundamental economic challenges. Earlier in life, most people are net savers, whereas after retirement they become net dissavers. As the latter group grows as a share of the population in the developed countries, households—together with the private pension plans they belong to and the businesses they own—will tend to save less of their aggregate income. The OECD projects that the private saving rate in the developed world could fall by more than half over the next three decades.

If the decline is anywhere near this large—especially if it is accompanied by mounting fiscal deficits to pay for these senior benefits—the result could be a global capital shortage, compounded by dangerously fluctuating interest rates, exchange rates and cross-border capital flows.

## A Look at Tomorrow's Economics

Whatever happens to savings, tomorrow's economies will look very different from today's. Older people, for instance, tend to consume more personal services and fewer manufactured goods.

On the plus side, this could open many new opportunities for business and economic growth. On the minus side, by accelerating the ongoing global trend toward services—where gains in output per worker are more difficult to achieve—it could act as a break on the developed world's productivity growth trend. On this score, we have not yet started to ask the right questions about what public policy can do to help raise productivity, and thus living standards, in an era when the economy will depend more on deploying at-home nurses rather than stamping out auto bodies.

Much hangs in the balance. By 2010, the work force in Japan younger than 30 will shrink by a stunning 25%. In most of Europe, work forces will be shrinking by roughly 1% per year, meaning that unless productivity increases at high levels, the real economies of some countries may begin shrinking as well.

---

## Entitlements Should Be Abolished

The case for abolition of Social Security and Medicare is overwhelming. They are fiscally ruinous and—in their redistribution from struggling young taxpayers to retirees—morally outrageous. Moreover, their taxes are crushing working people, especially self-employed young parents.

As for the need to save more and consume less, widespread entitlement abolition would force Americans to do this. It would also enable us to afford the tax relief that would give Americans the wherewithal to do that saving. There is no need for the tyranny and paternalism of forced saving.

Beyond radical entitlement curtailment, we need a revolution of beliefs. Benefits are forced on no one; they are paid because someone applies for them, out of a belief that he is "entitled" to them.

John Attarian, *World and I*, November 1996.

---

For at least a half-century, legislators and business managers have used expressions like "fiscal dividend" and "market growth" to refer to the natural tendency of tax revenues and sales to rise in a normal year. What happens, in this new environment, when one expects them to decline in a normal year? And if economies become a zero-sum game, will the positive trends associated with globalization be rolled back amid calls for greater protectionism?

Global aging is sure to breathe new life into the old debate over the pros and cons of population growth. Some economists stress that natural resources are finite and that less growth helps living standards and quality of life. Others note that fixed-cost undertakings become more affordable when that cost can be spread over a larger population and a growing economy. The classic examples are basic research and infrastructure investment. There will be new important examples of fixed-cost challenges. For example, in a world of escalating and varied national-security threats, will countries with shrinking populations and negative or limited economic growth conclude they cannot respond to these international challenges, to say nothing of making necessary public investments such as education?

In the years ahead, developed countries will look for ways to meet the needs of a growing number of elderly without overburdening the economy or overtaxing the young. My personal preferences are encouraging longer work lives, targeting benefits according to need, and transitioning from pay-as-you-go retirement systems to funded systems of personally owned savings accounts.

This last strategy does most to overcome one of the biggest economic challenges of global aging—namely, how to sustain adequate rates of savings and investment. Along with raising retirement ages, it also is the only strategy that allows elders to enjoy an undiminished living standard without imposing direct (tax) or indirect (familial) burdens on future generations.

Only one thing is certain: No country can afford to delay in addressing this issue much longer—at least if it intends to prosper in the [twenty-first] century.

> "[People] are poor not because of entitlement programs for the old, but because of private and public sector policies the elderly had nothing to do with."

# The Aging Population Is Not Hurting the Economy

Meredith Minkler

In the following viewpoint, Meredith Minkler contends that the elderly are wrongly blamed for problems in the American economy. She asserts that while programs such as Social Security and Medicare should be reformed, those programs are not causing poverty for younger generations. Instead, Minkler argues, economic problems are largely the result of corporate downsizing and government policies that benefit the wealthy at the expense of the middle and lower classes. Minkler is a professor of community health education and health and social behavior at the University of California at Berkeley School of Public Health.

As you read, consider the following questions:

1. According to Minkler, what percentage of its income does a family that earns under $38,000 per year pay in Social Security taxes?
2. How much of the wealth in the United States is controlled by 20 percent of the population, as stated by the author?
3. What is Minkler's suggestion for getting beyond the "villainization" of the elderly?

Reprinted, with permission, from Meredith Minkler, "Scapegoating the Elderly: New Voices, Old Theme," *Journal of Public Health Policy*, vol. 18, no. 1, 1997. Endnotes in the original have been omitted from this reprint.

A new class of people is being created. It is a revolution-ary class, one that is bringing down the social welfare state, destroying government finances, altering the distribution of purchasing power and threatening the investments that all societies need to make to have a successful future.

With these words, noted MIT economist Lester Thurow launched recently into a stunning indictment of the "class" most all of us hope one day to join: the elderly. Author of such highly acclaimed books as *The Zero Sum Society* and *The Future of Capitalism*, Thurow rails against a selfish and financially secure population block whose entitlement programs and single-issue voting are busting the budget and directly threatening the well-being of younger and future generations.

## Social Security and Medicare Are Not to Blame

We have, of course, heard this rhetoric before. But it typically has come from people like Republican financier Pete Peterson whose political interests are well served by finding in the old a scapegoat that helps deflect attention from the more fundamental causes of our economic problems. The Thurow tirade is important precisely because of the source: when a leading liberal economist and former editorial board member of *The New York Times* can make these statements and get away with them, we need to be concerned.

Few would deny that serious steps must be taken to reform Social Security and Medicare, ensuring the solvency of these programs while making sure that they don't cause undue hardships for the young. The gross inequities in financing for Medicare and Social Security also need to be addressed. It is outrageous that today, the median income family with earnings of under $38,000 pays close to 8% of its income in Social Security taxes, while the family earning 10 times as much pays under 2% and rich families with incomes 100 times the median, in the $4 million range, pay Social Security taxes at a rate of .01%.

But reforming Medicare and Social Security does not need to entail heaping blame on the elderly beneficiaries of these programs. Nor does it justify ignoring the facts. Poverty rates for the old, while certainly far lower than those for America's children, continue to be unacceptable: nearly

20% of older Americans are poor or near poor, giving the elderly the highest poverty rate of any age group except children. For almost half of the elderly poor, Social Security makes up over 90% of their income, while for those in the lowest socioeconomic status (SES) quartile, out-of-pocket health care expenses consume well over a third of their income. Finally, within the group increasingly portrayed as financially secure "greedy geezers" are large subgroups with very high poverty rates, among them many racial and ethnic minorities and women over age 85. And let's not forget those elderly poor who stand to get poorer still as a result of the draconian welfare reform bill. Or elders who have dared to remain noncitizens, and who now may face the loss of [Supplemental Security Income] (SSI) and most other federal benefits. Or the growing numbers of grandparents who are raising their grandchildren because of drugs, AIDS, violence or teen pregnancy, and who now face the loss of already miserly [Aid to Families with Dependent Children] AFDC benefits.

The image of the monolithic wealthy elderly frequently is accompanied by a second image—one of young families and children who are suffering as a direct consequence of our bloated programs for the old. Indeed, one recent *Newsweek* cover featured a young man being crushed under the weight of a heavy-set older woman in a wheelchair whom he was stoically attempting to carry. The problem, once again, is not with the argument that many younger people are suffering economic hardship and its consequences. Rather, the problem lies in the linking of this suffering with the old, and with their Medicare and Social Security "boondoggle."

## Corporations Have Increased Poverty

As the cliché reminds us, "children are poor because their parents are poor." And their parents are poor not because of entitlement programs for the old, but because of private and public sector policies the elderly had nothing to do with—with a few notable exceptions (Reagan and Bush Sr. come to mind). Corporate downsizing has erased more than 43 million jobs since 1980, and while far more new jobs have been created over this same period, fully two-thirds of full time workers who have lost their positions have ended up in lower-paying jobs. Many of the new jobs created have been at below-minimum wage, which still leaves a family of three well below the poverty line. Falling wages, a tighter labor market, and rising college costs have combined to such an extent that young adults today are in worse shape than at any time since the Great Depression. Finally and most compellingly, a quarter of America's preschoolers, and half of her African American preschoolers, live in poverty. These trends are a stinging indictment of our economy. But they are in no way an indictment of the elderly, or of Social Security and Medicare.

What about the popular argument, though, that Social Security is the "chief culprit" behind the budget deficit? As one *Fortune* magazine article recently put it:

> Want to put a face on America's persistent deficit and savings crisis? Forget those hoary clichés—the welfare queen, lazy bureaucrat, greedy businessman, weapons-crazed general or rich Third World potentate living off U.S. aid. Reach instead for a photograph of your Mom and Dad.

The argument is seductive. But it is also false. For like the rise in poverty in our nation's children, the tripling of the national debt from 1980 to 1990 had nothing to do with Social Security and little to do with Medicare. What it *did* have to do with, as Pulitzer Prize winners Donald Barlett and James Steele point out, was class warfare—a war which the rich and corporations won, and the poor and middle class lost decisively. When President Reagan came into office the top tax rate was 70%. When he left, it was 28%. And despite small subsequent efforts like the 1993 tax increase, the scales have remained heavily tilted in favor of the affluent. Fully 85% of all the wealth in this country is controlled by 20% of the population, and since 1980, almost two-thirds of earnings gains have gone to the top 1%. As Lester Thurow himself asks, "how far can inequality rise before the system cracks?"

The 1980s also saw a doubling of our defense spending, from under $150 billion to almost $300 billion a year. The decade witnessed, too, greatly accelerated tax breaks for corporations. In fact, it's been calculated that if corporations paid taxes in the 1990s at the same rate they did in the 1950s, we'd have enough money to wipe out two-thirds of the federal deficit overnight. Further, as Barlett and Steele remind us, the period of greatest reinvestment in America was not the 1980s, when corporations were reaping huge tax breaks, but rather the 1950s, when they paid fully 39% of total US taxes.

## Reforming Social Security

In making these points, I am not suggesting that we needn't make serious efforts to make changes in Social Security and Medicare. But I am suggesting that an analysis which blames Social Security and Medicare for our economic woes, and which would drastically cut these programs to turn things around, is sadly off the mark.

---

### Attacks on Entitlements

In one way or another, every budget-cutting attack on programs created to help the indigent, the disabled and the down and out impinges upon entitlements. Either the cost of entitlements is used to justify diminishing support to the needy, or continued funding of welfare programs for the needy is used to justify cutting entitlements. As part of the conservative backlash, Congressional leaders have been doing all they can to confuse "welfare" (temporary assistance to the unemployed and unemployable) with "welfare state" (Social Security and Medicare) in the public mind, two very different areas of policy that have different histories and goals. The aim of such deliberate obfuscation is to create the impression that seniors are living off "welfare" and should be ashamed to accept handouts. The very concept of "entitlement" is being called into question, as if to ask: Is anybody *entitled* to anything they did not earn in the marketplace?

Theodore Roszak, *Nation*, December 28, 1998.

---

As former Social Security commissioner Robert Ball points out, for example, relatively minor changes in Social Security could ensure the solvency of this program for many years to come. Such alterations might include having all revenue from the taxation of benefits credited to the Social Security trust fund; bringing state and local government workers into the Social Security system; computing benefits over 38 years instead of 35; and having more affluent beneficiaries pay taxes on any benefits that exceed what they paid into the system. No means testing, and no privatization of a system that is in fact meant to be social and not merely individual insurance.

The "great irony" of the calls to drastically revise the Social Security contract for the sake of younger Americans is, as policy analyst John Myles notes, that those who would be most negatively affected are *not* the old but the Baby Boomers and the Generation Xers: precisely those "who have already borne the brunt of almost two decades of market failure and rising inequality."

## Recognizing Interdependence

If we are to get beyond the media and the politicians' villainization of the old and of their entitlement programs, the misguided calls for justice between generations must be replaced by an approach to policy grounded in perceptions of our intimate interdependence. Such an approach will not be easy to sell, for in the words of ethicist Daniel Callahan, America "does not speak easily the language of community." As a nation, we have prided ourselves on rugged individualism, and as a polity, we shy away from moral consensus and argue instead that it's every person or group for themselves. We are taught at an early age that interest group politics are not only the way things are, but the way they should be.

The concept of intergenerational interdependence reminds us that a preschooler living in poverty, a young person faced with a low-paying job and unfairly high taxes, and an elderly woman with astronomically high out-of-pocket health care expenses are all part of the same picture. It reminds us, too, that that "photograph of Mom and Dad" will, before too long, be our own.

> *"The main way that older Americans can contribute is by doing the same thing that other adults do: that is, by working."*

# The Aging May Need to Continue to Work

Robert J. Samuelson

As the American population continues to age, steps may need to be taken to avoid putting too much strain on the economy, specifically on benefit programs such as Social Security and Medicare. In the following viewpoint, Robert J. Samuelson argues that one solution is for older Americans to stay in the workforce beyond the normal retirement age. He contends that people in their sixties and seventies should not be automatically entitled to government benefits and should instead continue to contribute to society through work. Samuelson is a columnist for *Newsweek* and the *Washington Post*.

As you read, consider the following questions:

1. What complications does Samuelson note regarding his suggestion that people work longer?
2. According to the author, what percentage of Americans aged sixty-five or older live in nursing homes?
3. Why was the retirement age originally set at sixty-five?

Reprinted from "Gray Dawn," by Robert J. Samuelson, *The New Republic*, April 12, 1999. Reprinted with permission from the author.

A ging societies around the world pose profound questions. Will they become economically moribund, because the old are less inventive and less accepting of change? How will families cope if people have to care for both their children and their parents who, increasingly, live to 85, 90, or 100? How will we deal with the ethical issues of prolonging life at great expense and little hope? Will the world become more dangerous, because older societies—with few children—will not risk their youth in war and will become vulnerable to those that will? [In his book, *Gray Dawn: How the Coming Age Wave Will Transform America—and the World*, Peter G. Peterson] poses all these questions and answers none of them, because they are unanswerable. We cannot predict the future.

## Changing Social Security and Medicare

But we are not powerless to affect the future. We can deal with the obvious problems. Many possible solutions are no mystery. In ["Raising the Earliest Eligibility Age for Social Security Benefits," January 1999] report, the Congressional Budget Office outlines some of them. One is to raise the eligibility ages for Social Security and Medicare. Already Social Security's normal retirement age of 65 is scheduled to move gradually to 66 by 2009 and stay there until 2020 (affecting those born between 1943 and 1954). Then it would rise slowly to 67 by 2027 for those born in 1960 or after. These increases could be accelerated. My own view is that we should move to 68 by 2015 or 2020, and then maybe to 70. Existing law would preserve Social Security at 62, though with reduced benefits. I would raise this threshold; and I would also raise Medicare's eligibility along with Social Security's.

Similarly, benefits could be skewed more toward poorer recipients. The existing formula already does this. In 1997, for example, it replaced 90 percent of new retirees' monthly earnings up to $455, but only 15 percent above $2,741. By tinkering with the formula, benefits in the upper half of the income distribution could be cut. The 65-and-over population also receives special tax breaks, mainly the exclusion of most Social Security benefits from taxes. In 1999, these [were] worth more than $20 billion. These should be phased out. And older Americans—especially the affluent—could be asked to bear more of the costs of Medicare. Today, Medicare premiums cover only about 11 percent of expenses.

Such proposals could be mixed in various combinations. Almost any plan would sharply reduce future budget costs. The Congressional Budget Office estimated that the savings from a more modest package (less increase in the retirement age, for instance) might keep the budget in balance over the next 75 years (assuming a constant level of taxes and other spending as a share of Gross Domestic Product (GDP)). But cutbacks also have a second purpose: to extend peoples' working lives by making earlier retirement less attractive. As Peterson writes: "Working longer is not a way to avoid the hard choices. It is the hard choice."

## Staying in the Workforce

Working longer does not mean that people will stay in career jobs for another three, four, or five years. Some will, but some will not want to—and some will not be able to. Corporate "downsizing" in the past decade hurt workers most in their late 40s, 50s, and early 60s. Companies in trouble are often in mature industries, and therefore have older work forces. Economic logic also induces companies to nudge out older workers, who are put at a disadvantage by seniority-based pay systems and fringe benefit costs. Peterson quotes the management consultant Sylvester Schieber: "In the U.S., we have a major problem in our pay structure being related to age. . . . Employer-financed health costs are higher for older workers. Leave programs award workers with longer tenures for time not worked. . . . Disability and workers' comp costs rise with age. All of these facets of the pay system reduce older workers' relative profitability."

So there are practical complications. If older workers have to be paid near the top of the pay scale, many companies will not hire them. Age discrimination laws need to take this into account. Nor should laws be drawn so tightly that companies can't dismiss workers who seem less productive or valuable. That would invite economic stagnation. Workers who lose career jobs—or quit because they are fed up after 20 or 30 years—may still need a job. But a new job may pay less than the old; and it might lack health insurance. Should people below 65 be allowed to buy Medicare coverage? If so, down to what age? At what price?

These practical problems, I think, can be overcome. The American economy has shown that it can generate new jobs and customize jobs to fit new groups of workers. Over the last 40 years, it has done so for two huge groups, women and teenagers, who have flooded the labor market. Why couldn't it do the same for older Americans? As labor-force growth slows—a consequence of societal aging—companies will surely seek to retain good workers. Firms might offer "staying" bonuses just as some now offer "signing" bonuses. Or they might design more part-time, part-year, or "consulting" jobs to accommodate a desire for more leisure.

## Important Questions Have Been Ignored

We do not really need to know the precise answers. If the economy remains healthy—if there is no depression—we can assume that the demand for older workers will materialize. But what about supply? Will older Americans want to work? Probably not, if we continue paying them so much not to work. Our present programs, which started as a humane effort to aid people who couldn't work and were inevitably dependent, now encourage them to stop working when they still can. Lower subsidies would reverse that. People would have to earn more to pay for their retirements. This is probably the only way that most Americans will work longer.

Hardly anyone discusses these questions. President Bill Clinton certainly is not discussing them. He has consistently refused to consider major benefits cuts—and he has attacked and undercut anyone who has considered them. His refrain is "saving" Social Security and Medicare. Congress, predictably, also will not touch the issue. Democrats regard Social Security and Medicare as political preserves. Republicans are terrified that any hint of a benefit cut (no matter how far in the future) will subject them to withering political attack. All the lobbies for older Americans protect benefits. And so there is a bipartisan consensus to do nothing. It could last for years, because the budgetary pressures of an aging society do not truly intensify for ten to fifteen years.

The problem with procrastination, of course, is that it will be hugely unfair to someone. As more people retire, it may be politically impossible to alter benefits. This would punish tomorrow's workers with higher taxes, lower government services, or higher federal debt. It is also possible that the costs of these programs will—when coupled with the impact of trends and events we cannot now foresee—become so heavy that Congress will be forced to cut benefits. This would punish baby-boom workers, who would have the rules of retirement changed in midstream, with little time to prepare.

## Older Workers Are Productive

When retirement took hold in the American mind, most work was physical in nature. It was obvious then that older workers were less productive than younger workers—they simply couldn't lift as many bales of cotton or carry as many bricks. Today the most physically demanding part of your job probably is pushing the buttons on your telephone or tapping on your keyboard. There's absolutely nothing that indicates older workers are less productive. In fact, most evidence indicates they're more productive.

When retirement was first being promoted, America had a large generation of young people that it had to absorb into the workforce. It made some sense, therefore, to open up spots. Today, however, the 20-somethings waiting in the wings are a small generation. They don't need to have lots of spots opened for them. In fact, there aren't enough of them to fill all the jobs [the baby boomer] generation is doing.

Stephen M. Pollan, *Saturday Evening Post*, May/June 1999.

President Clinton bears much of the blame for the present paralysis. One disappointment of Peterson's book is that he does not say so forthrightly. In 1994, Peterson served on the Commission on Entitlements and Tax Reform, appointed by Clinton. It urged action to curb spending, and Peterson blandly declares that "America's political leadership thanked us for the report, shook our hands, and walked away." No, it was Clinton who shook his hand and walked away. A President has the almost unique power to set the political agenda—to determine what issues will be debated, on what terms, and in what language. If a Democratic President will not acknowledge the need for benefit cuts, then Republicans will understandably shy away. When they bravely suggested cuts in Medicare in 1995, Clinton successfully—and dishonestly—savaged them.

Peterson writes as if he would still like to be invited to the White House. By soft-pedaling his criticism, he (and others like him) serve as enablers of this terrible procrastination. But there is a deeper cause of the present paralysis. Public opinion regards almost any discussion of cutting retiree benefits as inhumane, unprogressive, and even barbaric. Clinton panders to this climate and perpetuates it; but he did not create it. As long as it survives, debate will be stilled.

## An Outdated Image of Aging

The public's notion of aging subsists on an outdated image of retirees. Until now, I have depicted them as a cheerful, healthy, and secure bunch who frolic at everyone else's expense. This is wildly inaccurate, of course. A fifth of the 65-and-older population require some help in daily activities—dressing, getting about, eating. About 5 percent live in nursing homes. About 11 percent have incomes below the federal poverty line; and without Social Security, more than half might live below it. Older Americans have sharp and obvious anxieties. They fear loneliness, the death of a spouse, and the loss of self-sufficiency. They worry that they will become a burden on their children or that their children will abandon them. They dread going into a nursing home. They think about dying and the possibility that it will be prolonged, painful, and degrading.

Getting old isn't a picnic, but many of the worst medical and emotional problems do not occur until people reach their 70s or 80s. I have emphasized the opposite picture because it, too, is true—and it is ignored in our debates. We talk about old age as if nothing had changed since 1935 or 1965. . . . The retirement age of 65 dates back to [German Chancellor Otto von] Bismarck's pensions in the late nineteenth century. Yet political convention still considers this dividing line almost sacrosanct, pretending that everyone on one side is generally healthy, vigorous, and alert, and almost everyone on the other is frail, poor, and (sooner or later) feeble-minded.

We know from casual observation, common sense, newspaper stories (John Glenn rocketing into space), and research that this picture is false. And for those who distrust common sense or anecdotal evidence, the research is impressive. In 1987, the MacArthur Foundation began sponsoring an extensive study of the aging process by a variety of scholars. The results, summarized in *Successful Aging*, demolish the stereotypes. Here is one indicator of improved physical well-being: in 1957, 55 percent of the 65-and-older population had no teeth; now the figure is 20 percent. In general, the studies found that most people are physically and mentally fit well beyond 65. In 1994, 89 percent of those between 65 and 74 reported "no disability whatsoever." And the studies find that individuals' aging is affected more by lifestyle—diet, physical exercise, emotional connections—than heredity. (According to one study, the influence of genes is about 30 percent.)

It is long past time to conform political debate to social reality. We also need to reject the platitudes that the elderly can contribute to society by volunteering or offering "wisdom." This may be true, but it is a tiny truth. The main way that older Americans can contribute is by doing the same thing that other adults do: that is, by working, and not becoming a premature social burden. We need to abandon the notion that everyone over 65 is entitled to become a ward of the state. People do not suddenly become "needy" and dependent on their 65th birthday. I have always disliked the term "greedy geezers"—it is inflammatory and it stigmatizes an entire generation (mainly the Depression and World War II generation) for the good fortune of living long. But enough is enough. If baby-boom politicians perpetuate the status quo, we can be sure of one thing: our children will call us greedy geezers. And they will be right.

> "*Spending power is becoming progressively more concentrated among those aged 50 and older.*"

# The Aging Can Be a Powerful Consumer Force

Richard A. Lee

Americans in their fifties and beyond have significant economic power, Richard A. Lee asserts in the following viewpoint. According to Lee, a marketing consultant, these adults have substantial discretionary income that they often spend on their children or on the formation of new households after a divorce. In addition, Lee maintains that as these consumers age and become physically weaker, they are likely to devote their income to services that assist with tasks they no longer have the strength to complete, such as mowing the lawn or heavy lifting. He argues that advertisers need to target these consumers and not neglect the economic power of the aging.

As you read, consider the following questions:

1. What is the average discretionary income for people between the ages of 55 and 64, according to the author?
2. Why does Lee think "government-funded social-support services" do not completely solve the problem of marketing's neglect of older consumers?
3. What is the "driving force behind agency youth bias," in the author's opinion?

Reprinted, with permission, from Richard A. Lee, "The Youth Bias in Advertising," *American Demographics*, January 1997.

A youth bias in advertising is impeding normal development of a healthy and profitable market of goods and services for people in their 50s and beyond. Why do advertisers insist on directing messages to younger people to such an extreme that they deliberately turn off, blatantly insult, or merely ignore older consumers, who are becoming the economic mainstream?

## Fallacies About Older Consumers

Fundamentally, it's because selling the things that older people need and want in a way that entices them is not viewed as appealing, exciting, or rewarding. "Who wants to dumb down products for old people?" "Might damage our brand if younger consumers think we're for old people." "I'd never put an ad for 'seniors' in my book." And most telling of all: "Boooring."

How do these attitudes come about? The conventional wisdom in advertising tells us that household formation is something that people do in their 20s and 30s; so is buying homes, furniture, and appliances; so especially is buying clothing and supplies for babies and children; so is forming brand preferences that stick for life. Furthermore, families stay together and buy as a unit until children are grown, at which point they stop buying anything because they don't need much. Besides, older consumers buy the same brands over and over again, anyway. And lest we forget, the myth persists that younger people have money to burn and older people have to scrimp and save.

The unfortunate result of these fallacies is that they can potentially become a self-fulfilling prophecy. When older people see nothing directed at them, they gradually lose their sense of themselves as consumers, which dampens their consumer spending.

Some firms are shifting gears in appropriate directions. ServiceMaster is a national franchise outfit that has offered heavy-duty cleaning services to busy working middle-aged families for years. It is now branching out by deliberately marketing these same services to older consumers. It is also expanding into companion care services. But too many others have headed the other way, drilling down on younger

71

consumers like never before, in the hope that the youth market springs eternally profitable.

## The Spending Power of Older Consumers

It's hard to understand why advertisers still can't bear to tear their sights away from consumers in their teens, 20s, and early 30s, at a time when spending power is becoming progressively more concentrated among those aged 50 and older. Household income is highest for those aged 45 to 54. Households headed by people aged 55 to 64 have slightly lower incomes, but also fewer mouths to feed, giving them more buying power per person.

After everyone's been fed, clothed, and housed, the households that make out best in discretionary income are, surprise, these same ones, according to New Strategist Publications Inc. of Ithaca, New York. Not only are those aged 45 to 64 most likely to have any discretionary income at all, the 45-to-54 group has the highest average household discretionary income, estimated at $16,200 in 1994, while the 55-to-64 group has the highest per household member discretionary income, averaging $6,500 in 1994.

Older adults are also an increasingly diverse group of consumers whose needs are driven by their life stage as much as by their age. Some people in their 50s are forming new households after a divorce. Some in their 60s are still raising children and putting them through college. People who are involved with these typically "early" adulthood events at later ages usually have more money to spend on them.

Today's older consumers are sitting on a lot of that money, in part because they don't see enough marketing messages that persuade them to spend it. If they don't spend it before they die, their children stand to inherit billions of dollars. But even if they do spend it, the baby boomers who follow them will be an even larger customer base.

## A Growing Market for Social-Support Services

Among the costs of ignoring older consumers is neglecting the potentially huge market created by the weakening of people's physical condition over time. As early as our late 30s, most of us begin the long slide into physical frailty. Our bodies begin losing strength, agility, and durability. In our 40s, early arthritis, tendonitis, and vision problems kick in. By our mid-50s, many of us have trouble reading small print, and our long-suffering joints may force us to give up racquet sports. Managing a large lawn gets to be truly hard work, and shoveling the driveway may be ill-advised as our hearts begin to wear out. Chronic conditions like hypertension and diabetes become more prevalent. All this can happen before hitting age 60.

## Youth in Advertising

(percent distribution of total population, civilian labor force, and professional staff in advertising agencies aged 16 and older, 1995)

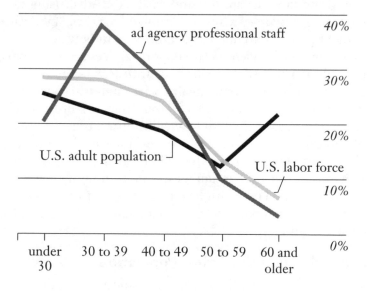

Source: High-Yield Marketing; Census Bureau; Bureau of Labor Statistics

The baby-boom generation may have bought a little extra time because it's learned that nutrition and exercise can delay the physical aging process to some extent. But boomers cannot infinitely put off the cold hard fact that their bodies are gradually losing steam. Just ask those who are already wearing bifocals and suffering from arthritis and back problems. Within a very few years, the oldest boomers will not be up to cleaning roof gutters or carting truckloads of debris to the dump, or helping their parents do these things.

Some boomers may have grown children or other young adults nearby to help them with these tasks. But many others will be looking for—and willing to pay—someone to install air conditioners when the weather gets hot and storm windows when it gets cold. Not only do they need the specialized tradespeople they've been using all along, such as plumbers, carpenters, and electricians; they also need someone to assemble the new grill with its tiny nuts and bolts and even tinier instructions. They need someone to rake the lawn. They need a trustworthy jack-of-all-trades to do the things they used to do themselves.

Not that things are better for those farther along the life scale, those in their late 60s and early 70s. Advertising targets younger people, while government services "take care of" older people. No one targets the ones in between.

Government-funded social-support services are an incomplete solution at best. They are mostly geared to the truly elderly who need in-home health care and transportation, rather than the "getting older" group that is still relatively healthy but needs help with heavy lifting and other chores.

Furthermore, government services don't begin to fill the void of recreational and other discretionary products and services that mature consumers would snap up if they were invited to do so. Help with heavy lifting is just the tip of the iceberg when it comes to the opportunities that an older population offers.

## Acknowledging the Aging Population

In the next ten years, the number of Americans in their 50s will grow over 40 percent. Most will be rediscovering the pleasures of a childfree environment. This doesn't mean they will revert to childhood themselves as "pop gerontologists" claim, or that they will stop spending money. It means they will be seeking sophisticated furniture, travel, food, and other things to reward themselves for the years they spent cleaning up grape juice spilled by youngsters and paying extra car insurance while saddled with teen drivers.

Product developers and distribution managers are belatedly starting to respond to the graying of our population and greening of older consumers' wallets. CBS learned its lesson by targeting the young and losing customers. The network is now refocusing its efforts on its mainstay audience of middle-aged and older viewers who prefer less sex and violence in their TV programming.

But advertising agencies barely recognize that buying power is migrating from families with children to empty-nest, pre-retiree, and retired households. They routinely resist setting their sights older.

This shouldn't come as a surprise. Advertising agencies today are largely populated by young people. This is particularly true of staff directly involved in creating advertising. Agency employment drops like a rock after age 40. As a result, agencies rarely have creative professionals with a true understanding of life after 40, not to mention life over 60 or 70.

This is not to cast aspersions on young people or agencies—it's simply the reality of human development. Some in their 20s and 30s do understand and appreciate the values and aesthetics of older generations. But most young agency staff, reflective of their life phase, are fixated on advertising that's hip, cool, impressive to their peers, and award-winning. This is more fulfilling than creating advertising for people with dated tastes who wouldn't know [musical group] Smashing Pumpkins if they stepped on them.

The driving force behind agency youth bias is a disconnect between agency demographics and those of the marketplace. Unresolved, this disparity will continue to cost sales. Agencies probably won't voluntarily address it. This would mean re-staffing, changing creative values, and generally retooling corporate culture. This is a difficult process to initiate internally, which leaves things up to agency clients.

## Ways to Target Older Consumers

Advertisers have two choices in overcoming agency resistance to targeting older consumers. They can stop using the agencies that persist in the practice. But this could be problematic at a time when advertisers are already shifting portions of their accounts to alternative agencies specializing in ethnic markets. Giving even more work to agencies that cater to older consumers would be tantamount to acknowledging that "primary" agencies are now secondary boutiques skilled in reaching only young white consumers. Most advertisers are unlikely to abandon traditional agencies to this extent.

The second option is to put external pressure on agencies to make the necessary corporate culture changes. This is a polite way of saying "use force" by threatening to switch agencies if that's what it takes to get serious attention for older consumers.

Those who persist in a youth bias are throwing boomerangs. What leaves their hands as slights and affronts to older consumers will ultimately come right back at them, in the form of lost business. Fortunately, corporate marketing executives don't die or quit at 40. They maintain hands-on involvement, especially in decisions about which customer segments should receive advertising attention, and how much. The best hope for the demise of an exclusive focus on youth in advertising is the marketing people who are growing and maturing themselves. They have the power to aim their advertising budgets more accurately. Let's hope they use it.

*"If you live long enough, independence inevitably becomes an illusion."*

# Aging Parents Will Need Help from Their Adult Children

Virginia Stem Owens

The loss of independence can make aging very difficult for both the elderly and their adult children, Virginia Stem Owens claims in the following viewpoint. She asserts that independence is considered the greatest virtue among Americans; therefore, it's difficult for the ailing elderly to accept that they can no longer care for themselves. Owens also contends that adult children often face the challenge of stepping in to care for their aging parents. She concludes that Americans must learn how to depend on others as they age. Owens is an author and a member of the editorial board of *Books & Culture*.

As you read, consider the following questions:

1. According to Owens, what proportion of people over the age of sixty-five live alone?
2. What makes middle-aged children skittish about caring for their parents, in the author's opinion?
3. In Owens's view, what cliché perpetuates the American worship of independence?

Excerpted from Virginia Stem Owens, "What Shall We Do with Mother?" *Books & Culture*, July/August 1999. Reprinted by permission of the author.

One day [in 1998], my father found my mother lying on the bedroom floor where she had fallen while tucking in a sheet. Her collarbone, they discovered at the emergency room, had snapped when she fell, an entirely predictable consequence of her combined ailments—Parkinson's disease and osteoporosis. Something else appeared to have broken in my mother as well, however. Confused and fearful, she took to wandering from room to room at night, looking for intruders. My father, 80 years old and profoundly deaf, felt helpless to deal with the rapidly deteriorating circumstances of their lives.

Since then, my husband and I have moved back to Texas and now live just down the road from my parents. During the past nine months, my father has had three operations, including a triple bypass. Between the two of them, they have seen a total of 12 different doctors over the past year. I have become an expert at reading medical billings, insurance claims, and Medicare statements. My computer's Web browser is bookmarked for a number of disease and medication sites. The learning curve for me has been Matterhorn-steep, however. At first I didn't even know the difference between Medicare and Medicaid.

My parents are scrupulous people who wanted to cause their children as little trouble as possible. Since I am the executor of their wills, they long ago gave me copies, as well as a key to their safety deposit box. They made sure I knew where to find their insurance policies. I was present when they planned and paid for their funerals. We had all prepared for death. What we hadn't prepared for was decline. I soon found that I needed a crash course in what is almost as inevitable as death—caring for aging parents. [Elizabeth] Kubler-Ross may have taught my generation the five stages of grief, but no one had told us about the long good-bye. . . .

## The Elderly Are Isolated

If industrialization isolated the elderly, where are they to find a foothold in today's electronic ether? In less than 20 years, from 1975 to 1993, the number of Americans over 65 who live with their adult children declined by half, dropping from 18 percent to less than 10 percent. There are doubtless many reasons for this decrease, from the improved health of older Americans to the number of two-or-more-job households. Nevertheless, a third of the over-65 population live entirely alone. One might expect the older that people get—and thus the more help they need—the more likely they are to live with one of their children. Just the reverse is true. If you make it to 85, the odds of your living alone jump to one in two.

I have noticed the tone of pride and satisfaction with which middle-aged children in America announce that their 80- or 90-year-old mother "still lives in her own house," as if voluntary isolation were the pinnacle of geriatric heroism. In other parts of the world, however, people would find this arrangement both strange and shameful. Most older people on this planet today live close to, if not in the household with, their children. At least until the last couple of decades, three-quarters of Japan's middle-aged children cared for their aging parents in their homes—almost eight times the rate in this country. In China, despite the deconstruction of traditional Confucian ethics by the half-century of communism, almost all old people still live with their sons' families. One researcher found only ten elderly people living apart from their families in a collective village of 40,000.

A bewildered delegate to a U.S.-China writers' conference once asked the American author Annie Dillard, "The old people in the United States—they *like* to live alone?"

## Obsessed with Independence

No doubt some of them do. Or at least some of them prefer living alone to the changes and compromises that living with others entails. Independence, is, after all, the chief and most honored virtue in this country. The ideal, ingrained in us early, persists even when we can, quite literally, no longer "stand on our own two feet." When our aging parents' need for help grows too obvious to ignore, we say they are beginning to "fail." Losing one's independence is, for Americans, a shameful thing. And needing help, we know, evokes in our potential benefactors pity, frustration, and fear—in roughly equal parts.

Independence. Autonomy. Isolation. On this unstable trinity the lives of older Americans are precariously balanced. But if you live long enough, independence inevitably becomes an illusion. Slowly the edges of your sovereign island start to erode. You can no longer keep up with the yard work, so you move to a condominium or even a retirement center. You can't see well enough to drive anymore. The checkbook gets tangled in knots, the Medicare maze impossible to negotiate. You call the pharmacy, and a computerized voice gives so many instructions about pushing phone buttons you hang up in despair.

Seeking help with these mundane chores of living means surrendering control as well. If you ask others to take you to the grocery store, you must fit your shopping to their schedule and preference for supermarkets. Rely on Meals on Wheels to deliver your dinner and you have to accept unfamiliar dishes. If your daughter volunteers to clean your house, you can't point out to her, the way you could when she was a teenager, the dust she missed. After a lifetime of doing and having things your own way, you may have to work at feeling—or even faking—gratitude.

## Caring for One's Parents

Of course, the fear of losing control of one's own life afflicts middle-aged children—my generation—as well. We are as skittish about pledging an unknown number of years to the care of our increasingly needy parents as they are about surrendering their autonomy. No wonder it typically takes a crisis to break through the stolid denial both generations erect to shield themselves from the obvious. A parent has a heart attack or a wreck, falls ill or just down, often in a distant city or several states away. You rush there, shocked not only by the disaster, but the deteriorated living situation. How could things have gotten so bad without your knowing about it?

You call your siblings, if they make reliable allies, and only then do you talk about what you're going to do about Mother or Dad. Despite the fact that this is one of the most predictable prospects you will have to face in your lifetime, no one has prepared for it. It comes as a complete surprise that Something Will Have to Be Done. Not next year, but next week. Or even tomorrow. You mentally inventory the entire family for the most flexible schedule, the most plentiful resources, the most compassionate or cooperative spouse. And no matter how much you love your parents and want to see them well cared for, you feel your own stomach clench as you try to imagine the future. Two sets of people, each with deep though unspoken fears and reservations, must now work out a way of dealing with a difficult situation. They will feel frightened, powerless, cornered, and overwhelmed. Their respective worlds are about to be turned upside down.

## The Responsibilities of Caregivers

The 1997 National Alliance for Caregiving/AARP National Caregiver Survey, which was funded by Glaxo Wellcome, revealed that 22.4 million households—which is nearly one-quarter of U.S. households—contain someone caring for an older relative or friend. Whether it includes intensive personal care such as bathing, dressing and feeding a parent or grandparent, or less intensive, everyday tasks such as grocery shopping, sorting out bills and insurance forms and transporting them to doctors' appointments, caregiving obviously involves a great many Americans.

On average, caregivers spend 18 hours a week caring for elderly relatives, and close to one in five provide what we call "constant care"; that is 4.1 million caregivers doing at least 40 hours a week of caregiving, unpaid.

Gail Gibson Hunt, testimony before the U.S. Senate Special Committee on Aging, September 10, 1998.

At this point, my parents live in their own home, but only because my father can still fix their breakfast, help my mother to the bathroom, and call for help if she falls. And also because I am nearby for emergencies—and to schedule and take them to their doctors' appointments, supervise their many medications, monitor their nutrition, and find suitable and reliable household help for them. During my daily visits I place their catalogue orders, pay their bills, deal with Medicare and their private insurance companies.

At night I lie in bed wondering how much longer my father's own precarious health—and strength—will hold out. What will I do if it doesn't? My parents' resources are not sufficient to hire round-the-clock nursing. I picture past scenes of my aunts and my own mother caring for their parents in their last days. And I remember that no one in our family has ever died—or lived—in a nursing home.

## Learning to Be a Burden

I still have many questions and quandaries about the future—my parents' and my own. But since coming back to Texas to help with my mother's care, I have at least learned not to repeat that oft-repeated cliché that undergirds and perpetuates our idolatry of independence: *I don't want to be a burden to my children.*

We are all, throughout our lives, a burden to others. From the moment of conception, we are nourished and nurtured by others. As adults we learn to pay for or negotiate our mutual needs, but the fact remains that it takes an invisible army of other people to grow our food, clean our clothes, maintain our roads, fuel our furnaces. When we marry, we accept another's pledge to stick with us in sickness and health, prosperity and poverty. The load we lay on others only becomes more visible, less deniable, as we age. Even though nothing is more predictable, Americans simply aren't much good at—and consistently fail to prepare themselves for—either bearing or being burdens. (As for wishing for a quick and trouble-free death that will cause our families no fuss or bother, only one in four of us can expect such an easy exit.)

Our still relatively new culture, which makes both living anywhere and living longer possible, will no doubt devote a good deal of public resources and private energy in the near future to figuring out how best to care for its older members. In the meantime, I will be moving into that category myself. Yet nothing in our culture to date encourages us to accept the reality of our future liability. Instead, we are enticed to believe in the Centrum Silver myth—that our latter days will be spent on cruise ships or jogging into the sunset, not alone but with our spouses. The truth is, though, should I live another 20 years, I *will* be a burden—to my spouse or my children or the state, if not all three. What I most want to learn during those decades, therefore, is not how to live longer, not necessarily even how to live a healthier or more productive life, but how best to be a burden. One that might also be a blessing.

# Periodical Bibliography

The following articles have been selected to supplement the diverse views presented in this chapter. Addresses are provided for periodicals not indexed in the *Readers' Guide to Periodical Literature*, the *Alternative Press Index*, the *Social Sciences Index*, or the *Index to Legal Periodicals and Books*.

Maria Sophia Aguirre — "The Graying of the Industrialized World," *World & I*, April 2000. Available from 3600 New York Ave. NE, Washington, DC 20002.

John Attarian — "Aging America's Fiscal Nightmare," *World & I*, November 1996.

Cathy Booth — "Taking Care of Our Aging Parents," *Time*, August 30, 1999.

David Callahan — "Still With Us," *American Prospect*, July/August 1999.

Patricia Chisholm — "All in The Family," *Maclean's*, January 17, 2000.

Lincoln H. Day — "Too Many (Older) Americans?" *Social Contract*, Fall 1999. Available from 445 E. Mitchell St., Petoskey, MI 49770.

Horace B. Deets — "Today's AARP," *Vital Speeches of the Day*, October 1, 2000.

Barbara Ehrenreich — "The Undeserving Old," *Progressive*, February 1999.

David Scott Johnson — "Economic and Social Conditions of Children and the Elderly," *Monthly Labor Review*, April 2000.

Theodore Roszak — "The Aging of Aquarius," *Nation*, December 28, 1998.

Sue Shellenbarger — "We Take Better Care of Our Elderly Parents Than Most Realize," *Wall Street Journal*, March 12, 1997.

Valentine M. Villa, Steven P. Wallace, and Kyriakos Markides — "Economic Diversity and an Aging Population: The Impact of Public Policy and Economic Trends," *Generations*, Summer 1997. Available from the American Society on Aging, 833 Market St., Suite 511, San Francisco, CA 94103-1824.

# CHAPTER 3

# Should Social Security Be Reformed?

# Chapter Preface

During the past decade, concerns have been raised that the U.S. Social Security system, which was established in 1935 as a way to guard the elderly from poverty, could go bankrupt unless it is reformed. One solution is privatization, an option adopted by Chile in 1981. Chile replaced its state-run system with one in which workers contribute between 10 and 20 percent of their income to pension savings accounts. Twenty private companies invest that money in mutual funds.

Bruce Bartlett, a senior fellow at the National Center for Policy Analysis, argues that Chilean privatization has been especially successful. According to Bartlett, most workers have earned a 12 percent rate of return on their investments. He also asserts that privatization has increased productivity and savings. José Piñera, who privatized the state pension system as Chile's minister of labor, asserts that the system is financially secure. He notes that rules require that funds are invested in a variety of stocks and bonds and that none of the companies that invest the pension funds have gone bankrupt.

Not everyone praises the Chilean system. In an article for the magazine *American Prospect*, Stephen J. Kay disputes the 12 percent rate of return cited by Bartlett. Kay writes: "[A] paper by World Bank economist Hemant Shah demonstrated that an individual's average rate of return over this period after paying commissions would have been 7.4 percent." Kay also states that barely half of Chilean workers contribute regularly to their pension funds. An article in the magazine *Labor Notes* cites other problems with privatization. For example, because women work fewer years than men and tend to live longer, they face "the danger of outliving pension savings." The magazine also asserts that privatization is expensive, costing three times as much to operate as the government-run Social Security system.

Like its Chilean counterpart, the American Social Security system has sparked considerable debate. In the following chapter, the authors consider whether the American system needs reform and whether privatization might be the best approach.

> "Social Security is not just a bad deal when the program becomes insolvent in 2013. It is a bad deal today."

# A Social Security Crisis Exists

Michael Tanner

In the following viewpoint, Michael Tanner argues that Social Security is a financially unsound program in need of reform. According to Tanner, a tax increase will be necessary by 2013 because the system will owe more in benefits than it collects in revenues. Tanner also asserts that Social Security is unfair to poor and minority Americans, who are among those most likely to benefit if Social Security is privatized—that is, replaced by a system in which individuals fund their retirement through private investments. Tanner is the director of the Social Security Privatization Project for the Cato Institute, a libertarian public policy research organization.

As you read, consider the following questions:
1. According to Tanner, what are the components of the Social Security trust fund?
2. What is the "democratization of capital," as explained by the author?
3. What is the value of Social Security's unfunded liabilities, according to Alan Greenspan and cited by Tanner?

Excerpted from Michael Tanner, "Ten Myths About Social Security," *Cato Policy Report*, July/August 1998. Reprinted by permission of the Cato Institute.

The debate over Social Security reform is heating up. As it does, we can expect the air to be filled with competing claims and counterclaims. Organizations from the AFL-CIO to the National Organization for Women have announced plans to mount a campaign against proposals to transform the 63-year-old retirement program to a system of individually owned, privately invested accounts. Therefore, it seems like a good idea to dispel some of the myths that you may be hearing. . . .

## Trust Fund Problems

*Myth 1: There's No Need to Rush; Social Security Is Safe for the Next 35 Years*

That rush of hot air you heard [in spring 1998] was the collective sigh of relief when the Social Security trustees reported that the system's technical insolvency date had been extended to 2032. But that date does not provide the full story of Social Security's looming crisis. The important date is 2012. Social Security taxes currently bring in more revenue than the system pays out in benefits. The surplus theoretically accumulates in the Social Security Trust Fund. However, in 2013, . . . the situation will reverse. Social Security will begin paying out more in benefits than it collects in revenues. To continue to meet its obligations, it will have to begin drawing on the surplus in the trust fund. Which brings us to

*Myth 2: The Trust Fund Is Real*

The trust fund is really little more than a polite fiction. For years the federal government has used the trust fund to disguise the actual size of the federal budget deficit, borrowing money from the trust fund to pay current operating expenses and replacing the money with government bonds—essentially IOUs. Half the trust fund consists of those bonds. The other half is simply an accounting entry attributing interest to the bonds.

The Social Security Administration insists that there is no need to worry. Those bonds are backed by the full faith and credit of the U.S. government. But that is irrelevant. Pretend for a moment that there were no trust fund. What would happen in 2013? The government would have to raise taxes to continue paying promised benefits. Now, consider what will happen with the trust fund. The government will have to raise taxes to make good on the bonds to continue paying promised benefits.

Either way, young workers can expect to get hit with a big tax increase.

## Social Security Is a Bad Deal

*Myth 3: Your Social Security Taxes Are Being Saved for Your Retirement*

Social Security is a pay-as-you-go program. The money that you pay in taxes today is not saved or invested for you in any way; it is immediately paid out in benefits to today's retirees. You have to hope that when you retire there is another generation of workers to pay the taxes that will fund your benefits. Unfortunately, because we are living longer and having fewer children, there are going to be fewer and fewer workers to pay taxes and more and more retirees collecting benefits. In 1950 there were 16 workers paying taxes for every person collecting benefits. Today there are just 3.3; by 2025 there will be only 2.

*Myth 4: Social Security Is a Good Deal for Today's Workers*

Even if there were no reduction in benefits or increase in taxes—an impossibility given Social Security's looming financing shortfalls—Social Security is an extremely bad investment for most young workers. In fact, according to a study by the nonpartisan Tax Foundation, most young workers will actually receive a negative return on their Social Security taxes—they will get less in benefits than they paid in taxes. Some studies indicate that a 30-year-old two-earner couple with average income will lose as much as $173,500.

That actual loss does not even consider the opportunity cost, what workers might have earned if they had been able to invest their taxes in real assets that yield a positive return. In fact, a study by financial analyst William Shipman demonstrates that, if a 25-year-old worker were able to privately invest the money he or she currently pays in Social Security taxes, the worker would receive retirement benefits three to six times higher than under Social Security.

That is one more reason why Social Security reform can't be

put off. Social Security is not just a bad deal when the program becomes insolvent in 2013. It is a bad deal today. Working Americans are losing money every day that they are forced to continue putting their money into a system that will cost them a substantial portion of their potential retirement income.

## Helping the Poor

*Myth 5: Well, at Least Social Security Helps the Poor*

The low-income elderly are much more likely than their wealthy counterparts to be dependent on Social Security benefits for most or all of their retirement income. In fact, the poorest 20 percent of the elderly receive more than 81 percent of their retirement income from Social Security. Clearly, raising the rate of return through privatization will help people with no income except Social Security.

In contrast, increasing payroll taxes to keep Social Security solvent would badly hurt the poor. The payroll tax is one of the most regressive of all taxes, a tax on wages. Seventy-one percent of Americans already pay more in payroll taxes than in federal income taxes. They can hardly afford the 50 percent increase in payroll taxes required to keep Social Security afloat.

In addition, the progressivity of Social Security is undermined by differences in life expectancy. Because the wealthy generally live longer than the poor, they receive more total Social Security payments over the course of their lifetimes. A February 1996 study by the RAND Corporation concluded that, because of differences in life expectancy, Social Security actually transferred wealth from the poor to the rich. The RAND study also concluded that the current benefit structure disadvantages African-Americans, who have lower life expectancies and marriage rates. According to the study, whites consistently earn higher rates of return than blacks. In fact, on a lifetime basis, the income transfer from blacks to whites is as much as $10,000 per person.

In a privatized system, an individual's benefits would not be dependent on life expectancy. Individuals would have a property right in their savings. Any benefits remaining at their deaths would become part of their estates, inherited by their heirs.

Privatizing Social Security would help the poor in another

Mike Thompson. Reprinted by permission of Copley News Service.

way, too. Today, after paying for the necessities of life and being forced to contribute 12.4 percent of their income to Social Security, few poor people have the opportunity to invest. But privatizing Social Security will make every worker an investor. The old distinction between capital and labor will come crashing down as every truck driver, waitress, and lathe operator becomes a capitalist, a stockholder. Sam Beard, a former aide to Sen. Robert Kennedy, calls this process the "democratization of capital" and points out that privatizing Social Security will give every American a real stake in our economic future. Beard also notes that the benefits are psychological as well as tangible. "Personal participation will make savings and economic education part of everyone's day-to-day experience. . . . The benefits of this knowledge for individuals and families will include increased economic capability, a confident sense of the future, and more power to make fundamental choices that effect their lives."

José Piñera, architect of Chile's successful privatization of its government-run pension system, explains that those types of changes took place in his country:

> The new pension system gives Chileans a personal stake in the economy. A typical Chilean worker is not indifferent to the stock market or interest rates. When workers feel that they own a part of the country, not through party bosses or a Politburo, they are much more attached to the free market and a free society.

The same worker empowerment is possible through privatization of Social Security in this country.

## Reform Is Necessary

*Myth 6: There Is a Legal Right to Social Security Benefits*

The fact that you paid Social Security taxes all those years doesn't mean that you have any right to Social Security benefits. The Supreme Court has ruled, in the case of *Nestor v. Fleming* (1960), that individuals have no right to Social Security benefits based on the taxes they've paid. Congress and the president can change or reduce Social Security benefits any time they choose. For example, Congress is currently debating whether to adjust the way the consumer price index (CPI) is calculated. If Congress were to adopt the proposal of the Boskin commission to reduce the CPI by 1.1 percent, the average Social Security recipient would lose $5,000 in lifetime benefits. Other suggested changes to Social Security, such as raising the retirement age or means testing, would also reduce benefits. And we should not forget that many Social Security benefits are simply taxed away today, a case of the government giving with one hand and taking away with the other. Increasing payroll taxes—as has already been done 38 times since the system's inception—produces similar results.

*Myth 7: Social Security Can Be Fixed with a Few Minor Reforms*

Defenders of the current Social Security system suggest that it can be fixed with only minor tinkering—tax increases or benefit cuts. But Social Security's unfunded liabilities are truly staggering—more than $9.5 trillion according to Alan Greenspan. Paying all the promised benefits, under the government's relatively benign intermediate assumptions, would require nearly a 50 percent increase in Social Security taxes, from 12.4 percent to 18.3 percent. That would be by far the largest tax hike in U.S. history.

*"Our economy is generating more than
enough income to provide a rising standard
of living for future generations while
meeting our commitments to Social
Security."*

# Social Security Is Financially Sound

Mark Weisbrot

Social Security is not in the midst of a financial crisis, Mark
Weisbrot asserts in the following viewpoint. Weisbrot maintains that people who seek to reform or reduce Social Security
are spreading inaccurate information. He argues that even if
the economy grows at half its current rate, there will still be
sufficient funds with which to pay the benefits. Weisbrot concludes that Social Security should be strengthened, not weak-
ened, because it aims to help everyone instead of only a fortu-
nate few. Weisbrot is the co-director of the Center for
Economic and Policy Research, an institution that promotes
democratic debate on important economic and social issues.
He is also the co-author of *Social Security: The Phony Crisis*.

As you read, consider the following questions:
1. According to a 1998 poll cited by Weisbrot, what
   percentage of adults aged 18 to 34 expect to receive
   limited or no Social Security benefits when they retire?
2. What is the main reason for the projected Social Security
   shortfall, as stated by the author?
3. In Weisbrot's view, who are the foremost foes of Social
   Security?

Reprinted, with permission, from Mark Weisbrot, "The Sky Isn't Falling—It's a
Phony Crisis," *The Washington Spectator*, March 15, 2000; for a subscription, write
*The Washington Spectator*, PO Box 20065, London Terrace Station, New York, NY
10011, or telephone 212-741-2365.

M ark Twain once said that a lie can get halfway around the world before the truth even gets its shoes on, and it's hard to find a more compelling example of that than the lies afoot about the security of Social Security.

## No Leaking Roof

In another analogy President Clinton has said that "we have a chance to fix the roof while the sun is still shining." With the economy growing and the federal budget balanced, he was talking about dealing with Social Security immediately. His audience was a regional conference on Social Security convened by the White House in Kansas City.

The leaky roof metaphor is illuminating, but we can make it more accurate. Imagine that it's not going to rain for more than 30 years—the time span that even the gloomiest forecasts call Social Security okay. And the rain, when it comes (and it might not), will be pretty light. And imagine that the average household will have a lot more income for roof repair by the time the rain approaches.

Now add this: most of the people who are saying that they want to fix the roof actually want to knock holes in it. Among other things, "reformers" have proposed privatizing the system, with individual accounts that could be invested in the stock market.

## A Financially Secure Program

That's the situation facing Social Security. It is well-known to those who have looked at the numbers that the program will take in enough revenue to keep all of its promises for the next 34 years without any changes. It's hard to think of any other program that can claim to be that secure.

Furthermore, the forecast of a shortfall in 2034 is based on the economy limping along at less than a 1.7 percent annual rate of growth—about half the rate of the previous three decades. If the economy were to keep growing at 1999's rate, as a matter of fact, the system would never run short of money.

But even if the dismal growth forecasts turned out to be true, and the program eventually ran a deficit, it would not exactly be the end of the world. The Social Security system would be far from "broke."

The program has promised, and historically has delivered, a benefit that rises with wages in the economy. To maintain this commitment we may have to increase the system's revenues at some point. Would this place an undue burden on the post–2034 labor force? Hardly.

Even if we were to increase the Social Security payroll tax to cover the shortfall, the added cost would barely dent 2034's average wage, which will be 30 percent higher than it is today. It takes a great deal of imagination to perceive this as some sort of highway robbery of today's youth by tomorrow's senior citizens.

Despite the fact that none of the numbers cited are in dispute, the public has been overwhelmingly convinced that Social Security is in deep trouble. According to a 1998 poll by Peter Hart Research, 60 percent of unretired Americans said they expected Social Security to pay much lower benefits, or no benefits at all, when they retire. The gloom was even deeper, at 72 percent, among people aged 18 to 34.

## Sufficient Economic Growth

The simple truth is that our economy is generating more than enough income to provide a rising standard of living for future generations while meeting our commitments to Social Security. That's true even at the slow rates of growth projected for the future.

The gains from economic growth are not as obvious as they should be, because the majority of employees haven't been sharing in them. Over the last 26 years, the typical wage or salary has stagnated in real terms. So when people hear that future generations will be able to meet Social Security's obligations because they will have a higher income, they don't believe it.

What this means is that reclaiming the majority's share of the economic pie is the real "challenge and opportunity of the twenty-first century," to paraphrase another of President Clinton's favorite lines. Yet the question of income distribution has been removed from the political agenda. Instead we are told that we will soon no longer be able to afford our not-so-generous social safety net for the elderly.

Ironically, the only real threat to Social Security comes not from any fiscal or demographic constraints but from the political assaults on the program by would-be "reformers." If not for these attacks, the probability that "Social Security will not be there" when anyone who is alive today retires would be about the same as the odds that the U.S. government will not be there.

## Confusing Medicare with Social Security

One of the tricks that Social Security's opponents have used is to fuse—and confuse—Social Security with Medicare. The idea is to lump the two programs together as "entitlements for the elderly." On the basis of the last 30 years of health care inflation, it is easy to project explosive growth in future Medicare spending.

But Social Security and Medicare are separate programs, funded by separate taxes. Most people probably do not distinguish between the part of their payroll tax that goes to Social Security and the part that goes to Medicare. But the two are financed separately, and they face very different financial problems from different causes.

According to the latest projections from the Congressional Budget Office, Medicare will be solvent without any changes for the next 20 years. However, if medical care inflation continues at its historic rates, Medicare will eventually run into trouble.

But this is less a result of the aging population than it is a problem of exorbitant price increases in our private health care system. Because the fees paid by Medicare to health care providers are overwhelmingly determined by the private health care system, Medicare's financial problems have been driven by decades of double-digit inflation in the private sector.

The current rate of increase in health care spending is economically unsustainable, regardless of what happens to Medicare. These projections make a good argument for health care reform, but they say nothing about Social Security.

[In 1997] Pete Peterson, a Secretary of Commerce in the Nixon Administration and head of the Concord Coalition, wrote a book titled *Will America Grow Up Before It Grows*

*Old? How the Coming Social Security Crisis Threatens You, Your Family and Your Country.* Peterson conjures up frightening visions of "a nation of Floridas." He foresees hordes of long-lived, gray-haired baby boomers jetting around the country on senior citizen travel discounts, laying waste to the potential Social Security savings of Generations X, Y, and Z.

The media have been influenced by these warnings. The *New York Times* has reported that "Social Security faces a crisis early [in the twenty-first] century when the 76 million in the baby boom generation start retiring and putting a strain on the system."

---

## Why Social Security Has Been Targeted

All this suggests problems ahead, but no crisis for a generation. WHY then are politicians sounding the alarm [on Social Security] so loudly? They are not worried about the *very* real health care crisis. The answer is *they see an opportunity to turn a government guarantee of security into a stock gamble.* Their not so secret formula is "privatization.". . .

Their campaign against "big government" is a drive to privatize the postal service, the prison system and any other government function that might produce profits under private enterprise.

Social Security is a major target. The thought of controlling the billions of dollars in the Social Security system has Wall Street drooling. To make this possible Congress will have to end Social Security as we know it.

Hayden Perry, *Against the Current*, September/October 1998.

---

The baby boomers begin retiring in 2008, and at that time Social Security will still be running an annual surplus of about $150 billion a year, in constant 1999 dollars. In fact, the last of the baby boomers will already be retired by the time the system suffers its projected shortfall at the end of 2034.

## A Mythical Time Bomb

It may come as a surprise to many readers that the main reason for this projected shortfall is not the retirement of the baby boom generation. The main reason is that people are living longer.

As people live longer lives they will have to decide how

much of their longer life spans they wish to spend in retirement, and how they plan to pay for it. But this is a decision that can be made by future generations. There is no reason for us to decide now that we must cut Social Security benefits based on anticipated longer retirements 60 or 70 years from now.

The Social Security trust fund lends its annual surplus, now running at over $100 billion, to the federal government. The surplus, which has been accumulating since 1983, when the payroll tax was increased, will help finance the baby boomers' retirement. That is why the program will not have any trouble meeting its obligations while the boomers are retiring.

So much for the "demographic time bomb" with which the system's "reformers" have been threatening us. With a few selected facts dressed up as surprises, such as a rising elderly population or a declining ratio of workers to retirees—not to mention an oversized dose of verbal and accounting trickery—opponents of Social Security have been able to create the impression that the program is demographically unsustainable.

## Social Security Guards Against Poverty

Social Security is our largest and most successful antipoverty program, keeping about half of the nation's senior citizens from falling below the official poverty line. It also provides about $12 trillion worth of life insurance, more than that provided by the entire private life insurance industry. The program's 44 million beneficiaries today include 7 million survivors of deceased workers, about 1.4 million of whom are children. Some 5.5 million people receive disability benefits, including not only disabled workers but also their dependents. For a typical employee, the value of the insurance provided by the program would be more than $200,000 for disability and about $300,000 for survivors insurance.

Social Security provides an inflation-proof, guaranteed annuity from the time of retirement for the rest of the beneficiary's life. The cost of retirement, survivors, and disability insurance does not depend on the individual's health or other risk factors, as private insurance does. And the benefits are portable from job to job, unlike many employer-sponsored pension plans.

The success of Social Security owes much to the superior economic efficiency of social insurance as a means of providing core retirement income. The program's administrative costs are a small fraction of those of the private alternatives. They amount to less than 1 percent of the payout, as opposed to 12 to 14 percent in the private life insurance industry. On strictly economic grounds alone, the case for Social Security is strong.

But social insurance also embodies a different ethic and a different conception of the relation between the individual and society. The ethic is one of solidarity, which is different from either self-interest or altruism. It transcends this dichotomy in favor of a collective self-interest that promotes the advancement of everyone.

Most of us will grow old and, either before or during that time, will experience health problems and reduced capacity for work. The ethic of social insurance says that "we are all in this together" and that it is in our collective and individual interest to pitch in and provide for these eventualities and risks. We can contribute when we are relatively young, healthy and working, and draw benefits when we are not.

Some will draw a luckier number in the genetic lottery. They may inherit wealth, or be more successful and healthy—and live longer—by virtue of their own efforts and wisdom. But this is no reason to deny the necessities of life to others, any more than we would want our local fire department to ignore calls from the poor, or even from those whose fires were caused by their own carelessness.

## Strengthen Social Insurance

Social Security has also become increasingly important in light of what has happened to the other two major sources of retirement income—private savings and employer-sponsored pension plans. Private pensions have shifted from defined-benefit plans to defined-contribution plans. In a defined-benefit plan, the employer assumes the risk associated with the financial return on accumulated pension funds by guaranteeing a specified benefit upon retirement. In defined-contribution plans, such as the 401(k), employees assume the risk.

All of this makes a strong case for expanding, rather than

shrinking, social insurance, especially if we want to counter the decades-old trends toward increasing inequality and poverty in the United States. Yet [1999 and 2000] have seen Social Security on the defensive as perhaps never before in its 65-year history. A number of political forces are responsible.

First and foremost are the Wall Street financial firms, with a multibillion-dollar stake in privatizing Social Security. They don't mind investing in the research and publicity campaigns of policy organizations that make it their business to convince people that the program is in trouble.

Then there are right-wing ideologues in Congress who have never reconciled themselves to America's largest antipoverty and social insurance program. And many liberals—including President Clinton—have found it useful for their own political reasons to pretend that Social Security needs to be "saved." Democrats have used an alleged Social Security crisis to fend off Republican tax cut proposals.

[Former] Republican presidential candidate John McCain has joined them on this issue, although both he and George W. Bush have also put forth partial privatization plans for Social Security.

Democrats also want to keep the issue of Social Security "reform" alive because it helps them at the ballot box.

The perpetuation of this charade diverts attention and potential resources from more important concerns. One-fifth of America's children are raised in poverty. We have 44 million people without health insurance and the numbers continue to grow, even at the peak of our longest-running business cycle expansion. Our educational system is failing to provide millions of children with even basic reading skills. And middle-class families are struggling to put their children through college.

It is well within our means to solve these problems. Most of them do not exist at anywhere near the same level in other industrialized countries of comparable prosperity. We are currently facing federal budget surpluses for as far as the eye can see. We should put these more pressing problems first on the agenda, and leave the phony crises for later.

> "*Privatization would enable workers to generate retirement income that is between 1.5 and 5.5 times greater than the Social Security benefits now promised.*"

# Social Security Should Be Privatized

Daniel J. Mitchell

In the following viewpoint, Daniel J. Mitchell contends that the current Social Security system cannot be fixed and should be replaced by private retirement accounts. According to Mitchell, such accounts would provide workers with significantly more income than they would earn through Social Security. He maintains that the poor would benefit the most if privatization were implemented because they would be better able to build a nest egg for retirement. Mitchell is the McKenna Senior Fellow in Political Economy for the Heritage Foundation and is the organization's chief expert on tax policy and related economic issues. The Heritage Foundation is a research institute that promotes policies based on the principles of limited government and individual freedom.

As you read, consider the following questions:

1. According to Laurence Kotlikoff, as cited by Mitchell, how much greater would retirement income be if payroll taxes were invested privately, compared to Social Security?
2. What options does the author provide for workers who want to receive the Social Security benefits for which they paid payroll taxes?
3. How have politicians discouraged personal savings?

Excerpted from Daniel J. Mitchell, "Creating a Better Social Security System for America," *Heritage Foundation Backgrounder*, no. 1109, April 23, 1997. Reprinted by permission of The Heritage Foundation.

There is no way to fix the current Social Security system, but there is a way to guarantee workers a safe and secure retirement. The answer lies in privatization, which has the added virtue of being relatively simple to implement. Younger workers would be allowed to pay the major portion of their current payroll tax burden into private retirement accounts, the money from which would be invested in stocks, bonds, and other income-producing assets (a portion of the tax could be retained to help finance benefits for current retirees and those nearing retirement). Upon retirement, these accounts would be exchanged for annuities that would pay workers a stream of income well in excess of the amount Social Security now promises to provide.

## Privatization Helps Workers

There is some truth to the old saying that it takes money to make money. Those with financial resources can save and invest their money and take advantage of compounded returns to increase their wealth. One of the strongest arguments for Social Security privatization is that it will allow low-income and middle-income workers to improve their financial stability in the same way. Instead of sending 12.4 percent of their income to the government, where it is spent immediately, low- and middle-income workers could elect to set aside some or all of that income in private retirement accounts.

These private retirement accounts would be completely different from Social Security. First, they would be private property; unlike promised Social Security benefits, income from private savings would not depend on the twists and turns of politics. Second, because their money would be invested in stocks, bonds, and other financial assets, workers would benefit from the real rates of return on capital, which have averaged more than 7 percent over the past 70 years (even including the Great Depression). Perhaps even more compelling, in any single 30-year period within those 70 years, the average rate of return did not fall below 6 percent. This obviously is far more favorable than the mediocre—or even negative—rates of return provided by Social Security.

Laurence Kotlikoff estimates that if payroll taxes were invested privately, workers' retirement income could be three times the amount promised by Social Security. The Institute for Research on the Economics of Taxation (IRET) has found that private investment would allow a worker to retire with five times as much as Social Security can provide (and more than seven times as much as it can afford). Put another way, the retirement income a worker can generate by privately saving only 2 percent of current income is greater than the amount the same worker can receive in exchange for taxes now sent to Social Security.

Similarly, Martin Feldstein has concluded that contributing 2.5 percent of income to a private savings account would provide the same benefits as one receives in exchange for the full 12.4 percent payroll tax sent to Social Security. According to a National Chamber Foundation study, the couple with average income who started working in the mid-1980s would retire with more than $1 million if they had been free to save privately what they now pay to Social Security—even if financial markets performed only half as well as the historical average. Economists at Texas A&M University have concluded that privatization would enable workers to generate retirement income that is between 1.5 and 5.5 times greater than the Social Security benefits now promised.

## Benefits for Older Workers

Almost all analysts agree that younger workers would be better off with a private system, but some are concerned that older workers, because they are trapped in Social Security, would not be able to profit from privatization. This view is mistaken. Private savings accounts could be set up for workers at any stage of their careers, with benefits dependent on the number of years remaining until retirement. The only real issue is how to account for all the payroll taxes workers have been sending to the government all these years.

Depending on their circumstances, some workers would be so much better off under a private system that they could quit Social Security today and still come out ahead. . . . Exactly when workers could leave Social Security profitably without receiving anything in exchange for their taxes depends on three factors: sex, marital status, and income.

Even though many workers would do better by walking

away from Social Security and writing off the taxes they have paid into it (and even though they might be happy with such an opportunity), such an approach might appear to be unfair. If workers have been forced to pay into the system for years, they should receive something in return. Moreover, many would be too old for a "cold turkey" approach. There should be a way to allow workers to enjoy the benefits of privatization without losing the value of the payroll taxes they have paid into the system.

## Age at Which an Individual Could Abandon Social Security and Still Come Out Ahead

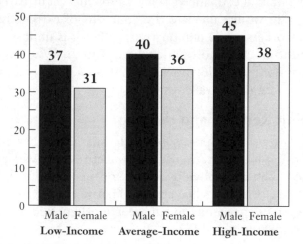

Note: After going "cold-turkey," amount of payroll tax is invested in a private retirement savings plan. All money contributed to Social Security is lost, and no Social Security benefits are received. This opt-out is hypothetical, as current law prohibits this action.

Source: Tax Foundation.

Fortunately, there are two reasonably simple ways to do this. The first would be to create a dual system. Workers could leave Social Security and, upon retirement, receive a monthly benefit check from the government based on their earnings and the amount of taxes they paid into the system before privatization. The bulk of their retirement income, of course, would come from private savings accounts set up after privatization.

The second option also would allow older workers to set up private savings accounts. Instead of maintaining a dual system, however, the government would give workers a rebate reflecting the value of what already had been paid into the system. This rebate, probably in the form of a bond that would mature upon retirement (as is done in Chile), would become part of the private savings account. A vast majority of workers would benefit under this approach.

Finally, workers should have the option of remaining in the current Social Security system. Although such a decision would not make financial sense, allowing them to choose this option would alleviate the concerns of extremely risk-averse workers while demonstrating that it is impossible for anyone to be worse off under privatization. When this option was used in Chile, more than 90 percent of workers still chose to join the private system.

## Helping Retirees and the Poor

All privatization proposals explicitly guarantee that benefits for those who are retired or near retirement will not be touched. The most obvious reason for this is political. Social Security reform looks like an uphill battle as it is, and it is almost certain that antagonizing existing beneficiaries would make reform impossible.

There is also a moral argument that favors preserving the status quo for senior citizens. Simply stated, the government made a contract with them to provide a certain level of benefits in exchange for taxes paid, and it would be wrong to break that contract. Some critics note that older retirees are getting much more from Social Security than they paid in, but that argument would have been worth making when the system was first created. To renege on the deal now would disrupt the lives of millions of recipients who have assumed that the government would honor its word.

Although privatization generally is a win-win proposition, some groups will receive disproportionately better benefits. Among the biggest winners would be the poor. More than any other group, lower-income Americans rely on Social Security for their retirement income. For the poorest 20 percent of the elderly, it represents more than 80 percent of their income. A private system that allows the poor to build a nest egg of savings for retirement also will give them greater and more secure income when they retire. The benefits for the poor are even clearer when one considers that, according to the Social Security Administration's (SSA) own figures, future tax collections will be sufficient to pay only 70 percent of future benefits.

Defenders of the current system argue that Social Security is still a reasonably good deal for lower-income workers because calculations of monthly retirement checks are skewed to help the poor replace a greater share of pre-retirement income. The fact that rates of return for middle- and upper-income workers are worse than the rate of return for lower-income workers, however, does not mean that the poor would not be better off in a system based on private savings, especially when one considers that life expectancies vary with income. The poor generally do not live as long as those with higher incomes, and therefore also do not live long enough to collect as much in Social Security benefits. Moreover, because benefits depend on only 35 years of wages, those who work for longer periods get absolutely nothing in exchange for the additional payroll taxes they have paid. Needless to say, the biggest victims are the poor, who work longer than those with higher incomes, largely because they spend fewer years in school.

The poor also stand to reap additional benefits from privatization. Specifically, they are the most likely to benefit from the increased economic growth and job creation that would follow a shift from a tax-based entitlement program to a savings-based private savings plan.

## Privatization Will Increase Savings

One of the big benefits of privatization is the positive impact it would have on the rate of savings in the United States. A global study conducted by the World Bank found that government systems undermine savings, and this conclusion is confirmed by the U.S. experience. Analysis of household behavior in the United States indicates that every dollar of perceived Social Security benefit reduces private savings by 60 cents. Even a study co-written by a researcher at the SSA confirms that "a dollar of Social Security wealth substitutes for about three-fifths of a dollar of fungible assets." Privatization would reverse this corrosive effect, replacing a system that drastically reduces savings with an approach based on real savings.

The rate of personal savings in the United States is among the lowest in the world. Not only does the U.S. government punish the frugal by double taxing (and sometimes triple taxing and quadruple taxing) savings and investment income, but politicians have eliminated most of the reasons to save. The subliminal messages being sent out are (1) that saving for retirement and health care expenses is unnecessary because the government will tax someone else to give you money when you get old in addition to providing you with Medicare and Medicaid benefits; (2) setting aside money for education is not necessary because the government is picking up more and more of the tab; and (3) buying a house will not be difficult because the government has numerous ways to subsidize the purchase.

Privatization of Social Security might not address all of the government's anti-savings policies, but creating private retirement accounts based on real savings would be a step in the right direction.

> *"We need a plan that . . . resists even partial privatization, reminds Americans just why Social Security is so legitimately valued, and shores up its finances."*

# Social Security Should Not Be Privatized

Robert Kuttner

In the following viewpoint, Robert Kuttner contends that privatization is not the best way to reform Social Security. Kuttner maintains the proponents of privatization overstate the yields that would be accrued through private investments and seek to destroy the political coalition that supports Social Security. He suggests that Social Security should instead be supplemented by endowment accounts—money that would be given by the government to children when they are born and that would be available for education, home ownership, and retirement. Kuttner is the founder and co-editor of the magazine *American Prospect*.

As you read, consider the following questions:
1. Why does Kuttner argue that comparing stock market returns and Social Security returns is like comparing apples and oranges?
2. How would the author finance his proposed endowment accounts?
3. In the author's view, how would the endowment account approach restore a "politics of generational alliance"?

Excerpted from Robert Kuttner, "Rampant Bull," *The American Prospect*, July/August 1998. Reprinted with permission.

There are four basic criticisms of [Social Security] privatization plans. First, they are not a solution to the real financial shortfall, but merely an opportunistic run at changing the system, taking advantage of concerns for its long-term solvency. By definition, any plan that diverts revenues currently dedicated to Social Security payouts only increases the shortfall. All of the privatization advocates who have faced this problem honestly have called either for tax increases, increased borrowings, or benefit cuts. But if such new taxes or borrowings were simply allocated to the present Social Security system, its shortfall would be solved. Indeed, as I will suggest, there are far better uses of new taxes to finance social insurance.

## Further Criticisms

Second, any comparison of stock market returns with Social Security returns compares apples with oranges. Social Security is far more than just a pension system, and its payouts are government guaranteed. It is also deliberately redistributive. More than three-fifths of retired Americans derive at least half their income from Social Security; without it, half would live in poverty. Dedicating some of the payroll tax to a private account system would divert that much revenue into a system that is neither redistributive nor government guaranteed.

Third, the promise of higher yields through investment in equities is overstated and in any case does not require individual accounts, with all of the risk and overhead expense that change would entail. Administration of such accounts and broker profit would consume 10 to 20 percent of the benefits. If we as a society think Social Security reserves should be partly invested in the stock market, the system can do that—collectively—at lower cost and at lesser risk than if private stock fund managers are given the job.

Fourth—and the right surely understands this all too well—breaking Social Security into individual accounts would explicitly segregate the system's antipoverty component from its contributory aspect and thus erode the political coalition that now supports its solidaristic and universal character. Writing in 1985, in a Cato book edited by Peter

Ferrara titled *Social Security: Prospects for Real Reform*, Stuart Butler laid out what became the right's privatization strategy. In creating individual retirement accounts, Butler wrote:

> The final element of the strategy must be to propose moving to a private social security system in such a way as to detach, or at least neutralize, segments of the coalition that supports the existing system. A necessary step towards this objective is to honor all outstanding claims on the existing system. [Otherwise] the retired (or nearly retired) will strongly oppose any package that threatens to significantly reduce their benefits.

This strategy, of course, is exactly what the right has pursued. Butler couldn't have imagined he'd have Pat Moynihan as his paladin. Privatization, by design, would lead inexorably to more privatization, leaving a means-tested, underfunded welfare system as a rump.

## Defending Social Security

In part, this is a debate about how many tiers of a retirement system we need and how to structure and finance them. Social Security was never intended to be the whole system. "Above" it are personal savings, Individual Retirement Accounts (IRAs), Keoghs, 401 (k)s, and private pension plans, all of which explicitly reflect earnings during working life. "Below" it are means-tested forms of aid for the very poor, such as supplemental security income (SSI). The system is unraveling both above Social Security and below it. Fewer Americans have employer-provided pensions; according to Brookings Institution economist Henry Aaron, only 3 percent of moderate-income Americans have IRAs; and means-tested social aid is declining in real, inflation-adjusted value. Social Security is the only part of the system that is universal and guaranteed.

Defenders of social insurance face an epic decision that is both philosophical and tactical. Do they stick to the "nip-and-tuck" script, run a public education campaign, and hope that the system's residual popularity carries the day? With every defection of a leading Democrat and with the escalating mismatch of lobbying resources, this course becomes ever less credible. Or do they try to outflank the right with something bold and new?

Here, liberals need to fight on two fronts. For the short

run, we need a plan that challenges the crisis rhetoric, resists even partial privatization, reminds Americans just why Social Security is so legitimately valued, and shores up its finances. . . . At the same time, the right has touched a popular chord with its proposals to allow the young to accumulate wealth. And the right's disinformation campaign has done serious damage to public confidence in Social Security. We do need something that builds real wealth, starting when people are young, and that expands the tacit intergenerational aspect of Social Security into something more tangible. The right, having opened the door to tax increases to finance their pet individual accounts, invites liberals to respond in kind with something bolder and more effective. This initiative should not substitute for a vigorous defense of the present system, which must remain as a centerpiece, but serve as a complement—to revive first principles, stimulate debate, and engage the young.

## The Endowment Account Solution

One big idea that might steal the right's clothes is a new system of what I have termed endowment accounts. Different versions of this have been proposed by Yale Law Professor Bruce Ackerman on the left, and pamphleteer Sam Beard and House Budget Committee Chairman John Kasich and Senate Finance Committee Chairman William Roth on the right.

In Ackerman's version, every American child would get $80,000 at birth, financed by a tax on wealth. In the Kasich and Roth versions, the budget surplus would finance a new system of individual retirement accounts. What differentiates the Kasich and Roth plans from other conservative proposals is that they would not divert any of Social Security's current revenue stream. Their plans, however, are unattractive on three grounds. The sums are puny; the finances are entirely dependent on the budget surplus; and there is no intergenerational dimension—only more retirement accounts. Still, it is noteworthy that two influential conservative Republicans have proposed a (modest) form of wealth redistribution—since everyone would get the same annual benefit, financed from general tax revenues. So a door has been opened.

In my version of the proposal, every American child would

get $5,000 at birth. The money would be administered by the Social Security system and invested collectively in bonds and stock index funds but accounted individually. In other words, each American child would have a nest egg, of real wealth. For low-income children, the government would add $1,000 every year of childhood. Middle-income families would get a tax deduction for annual contributions of up to $1,000 per child. If a child's account received $1,000 for each additional year of childhood, with normal investment returns and compounding, about $50,000 would accumulate by the time the child turned 18.

---

## The Danger of Bear Markets

For most people, saving for retirement is concentrated during the last 20 years of their working lives. While some people will be lucky, and be saving during periods when stocks are booming, others will be unlucky and have their prime saving years wiped out by bear markets.

The nation's confidence in stocks may be high because of the great bull market stretching from August 1982 through the present. But during the four 20-year periods in this century—1901–1921, 1929–1949, 1962–1982, and 1964–1984—average stock returns (in real terms, corrected for inflation) were close to zero, or worse. This means, for instance, that investors purchasing stocks in 1929 and holding them for 20 years would have lost money on their investments by 1949.

Richard B. Du Boff and John Miller, *Dollars and Sense*, May/June 1999.

---

Under my proposal, half of this accumulated money could be spent on college tuition, at age 17 or afterward. At age 30 or beyond, two-thirds of the residue could be spent on home ownership and/or lifetime education and job training. A tax deduction would continue to be available for modest annual contributions into the fund. Beginning at age 60, the residue could be withdrawn to supplement other savings for retirement. What remained could be passed along to heirs. This program, of course, is explicitly redistributive where Social Security is tacitly redistributive. But it builds on the tradition of universal free public education, the Homestead Acts, the GI Bill, and subsidized home loans—all programs through which society as a whole helps young people into the middle class.

## The Benefits of Endowment Accounts

This program of endowment accounts, which would cost on the order of $50–75 billion a year, could be financed by the projected budget surplus, supplemented by a lifting of the cap on income subject to Social Security tax and a surtax on very large incomes and estates. Unlike most proposals on the table, it would supplement rather than supplant Social Security. The proposal outflanks the right in several attractive respects.

First, it addresses the liberal goal of helping people of modest means to accumulate real wealth rather than just accounting claims against the Treasury. This is an idea the right appropriates—State Street Bank CEO Marshall Carter speaks loftily of helping working people accumulate wealth—but because there is little redistribution in most conservative versions, the real transfers to people of modest means turn out to be paltry. With the exception of Kasich and Roth (which are puny) and Beard (which diverts money from Social Security), all of the leading conservative plans base contributions to the proposed individual accounts on the pattern of an individual's earnings. This feature, of course, sacrifices the redistributive aspect of Social Security. And the more that individual accounts replace Social Security, the more redistribution and antipoverty effects are sacrificed. Endowment accounts, by contrast, would be highly redistributive. They would likely increase the national savings rate—but progressively.

More importantly, the endowment account approach accomplishes two other things of great strategic importance. First, it restores a politics of generational alliance. Young people are skeptical about Social Security in part because most have to wait decades to get tangible benefits. A system of endowment accounts would provide benefits throughout the life course. Further, it would entrust management of this new system precisely to the Social Security program rather than to thousands of private Wall Street middlemen—thus reinforcing the public system and its political support and ideology. Social Security would remain the centerpiece of a multitiered system. Compared with other nations, our Social Security program is already too meager. The ratio of U.S. Social Security benefits to pre-retirement income ranks tenth out of eleven advanced nations. It makes no sense to cut the program back further.

But it does make sense to supplement Social Security, both as a matter of equity and of politics. Far better than just playing defense, we need a grand debate about how to complement Social Security, based on first principles and ultimate ends. A new, wealth-broadening, intergenerational compact should be the high ground of that debate. To effectively defend Social Security, we need a bolder intergenerational compact—worthy of the liberal imagination that gave us social insurance more than 60 years ago.

*"Virtually every woman . . . would probably be better off financially under a system of fully private, personal retirement accounts."*

# Women Will Benefit If Social Security Is Privatized

Darcy Ann Olsen

In the following viewpoint, Darcy Ann Olsen argues that Social Security is unfair to women and should be replaced by a private system in which payroll taxes are placed in personal accounts. Olsen asserts that because women tend to work fewer years and earn lower wages than men, they receive less in Social Security benefits. She also argues that the rules are further biased against working wives because married women are permitted to collect either their own benefits or their spousal benefits, but not both. Olsen concludes that virtually all women, regardless of marital status or income, will be better off under privatization. Olsen is the director of education and child policy at the Cato Institute, a libertarian public policy organization.

As you read, consider the following questions:

1. According to law, to what percentage of a husband's Social Security benefits is a wife automatically entitled, as stated by the author?
2. What was the average monthly Social Security benefit for men and women in 1995, according to Olsen?
3. According to the author, how much more will women earn in a fully privatized system, as compared to their projected earnings under Social Security?

Excerpted from Darcy Ann Olsen, "Greater Financial Security for Women with Personal Retirement Accounts," *Cato Institute Briefing Papers*, July 20, 1998. Reprinted with permission from the Cato Institute.

Plans to privatize Social Security—that is, to redirect payroll tax payments into personal accounts similar to individual retirement accounts or 401(k) plans—have become enormously popular. Polls show that a large majority of Americans favor some amount of privatization. Democratic and Republican legislators have introduced bills that would privatize the system to varying degrees. And experts of various ideological persuasions have endorsed privatization. Yet many questions about privatization remain, particularly with regard to women. Would poor women be able to weather market downturns? Would they be capable investors? What about women's aversion to risk?

Many people agree that a retirement system should address poverty among the elderly. That, after all, was the primary reason for establishing Social Security. Unfortunately, the current Social Security system does not adequately address poverty among the elderly, particularly elderly women. Although the current Social Security system does not differentiate between men and women, on average, women receive lower benefits than do men. That is primarily because women tend to have lower wages and fewer years in the workforce. Thus, poverty rates are twice as high among elderly women as among elderly men: 13.6 percent compared to 6.2 percent. Although Social Security alleviates some poverty, clearly there is room for improvement.

In contrast, research shows that virtually every woman—single, divorced, married, or widowed—would probably be better off financially under a system of fully private, personal retirement accounts, the earnings of which could be shared by spouses. And the greater the contribution rate, the greater the financial security. Thus, a fully private system with a 10 percent contribution rate would benefit women more than a partly private two-tiered system. That is true even for poor women who move in and out of the job market.

## Social Security Is Unfair to Women

By law, the Social Security system treats all workers equally. Yet the system has a disparate impact on women because they typically earn less, work fewer years, and live longer than do men. In particular, Social Security punishes married women who work and favors married women who do not work. A married women who works her entire adult life may not receive any more benefits than a married woman who has never worked; a couple with two breadwinners may get fewer benefits than a couple with one breadwinner and identical lifetime earnings, and widows of two-earner couples may get less than widows of one-earner couples.

Those inequities result from the way benefits are calculated. A spouse can receive benefits in one of three ways. First, she can receive benefits based on her own work history. Second, she can receive benefits based on her husband's work history. By law, a woman is automatically entitled to benefits equal to 50 percent of her husband's benefits, whether or not she has ever worked or paid Social Security taxes. Third, she can receive benefits based on a combination of the two.

When a woman qualifies for benefits both as a worker in her own right and as a spouse (or surviving spouse) of a worker, she is subject to the "dual entitlement rule." That rule prevents her from collecting both her own retirement benefit and her spousal benefit. Instead, she receives only the larger of the two. And because the typical woman earns less and works fewer years than her husband, 50 percent of her husband's benefits is often larger than the benefits she would be entitled to receive in her own right. Consequently, she receives benefits based on only her husband's earnings—she receives no credit or benefits based on the payroll taxes she has paid. A woman who never worked at all receives exactly the same benefits.

## The Dual-Entitlement Rules Reduces Benefits

The second inequity that results under Social Security's dual-entitlement rule is that a couple with two breadwinners may get fewer benefits than a couple with one breadwinner and identical lifetime earnings. . . .

While the dual-entitlement rule has a negative impact on many two-earner couples during their retirement years together, its most pernicious impact is often felt after a husband dies. Social Security's survivor benefit rules can leave widows with up to 50 percent less income than the couple was receiving when the husband was alive. That is one reason why the poverty rate among widows is 19.2 percent, two times greater than among widowers. And, in general, the *more* of the couple's earnings the widow earned, the *smaller* the share of the couple's retirement benefit she receives after her husband dies. . . .

---

## Misguided Faith in Social Security

Advocacy groups such as the National Organization for Women . . . are portraying the proposals to replace the current Social Security system with a system of individually owned retirement accounts as dangerous to women. Long on criticism and short on solutions, their faith in the current Social Security system is misguided. More than 60 years after its founding, and with the original program's basic structure intact, the government's retirement system has not kept pace with today's modern women.

Naomi Lopez, *San Diego Union-Tribune*, December 13, 1998.

---

Anna Rappaport of William M. Mercer found that the situation for low-income widows who worked is even worse. For example, the wife of a couple with $34,200 in annual pay gets $1,082 as a widow if she never worked, while the wife who brought home half that paycheck gets a widow's benefit of only $674. That is a difference of $408 per month.

The Social Security Administration reports that 24 percent of married and widowed women have their benefits slashed by the dual-entitlement rule. That number is projected to increase to 39 percent by 2040, as increasing numbers of women earn higher wages and work more hours. As Jonathan Barry Forman, former tax counsel to Sen. Daniel Patrick Moynihan (D-N.Y.), puts it, "In short, the Social Security system takes billions of payroll tax dollars from these working women and gives them no greater Social Security benefits in return."

The negative impacts of the dual-entitlement rule are exacerbated by a handful of other factors that make women disproportionately dependent on Social Security benefits. As a result of lower earnings and fewer years of work, women, on average, earn less Social Security benefits than do men. In 1995 male retirees received $810 in monthly benefits while women received only $621, on average. Lower earnings and part-time employment also make it more difficult for women to accumulate private savings for retirement. In addition, women are less likely than men to have employer-provided pension plans. Even if they do have pension plans, they generally save too little because of their moves in and out of the job market.

Those gender-specific issues aside, women, like men, face the larger problem of Social Security's looming debt and declining rate of return. Federal Reserve Board chairman Alan Greenspan estimates that Social Security's unfunded liability is roughly $9.5 trillion. If the government intends to make good on its promise to pay retiree benefits, it will have to raise taxes or cut benefits in order to meet that revenue shortfall. The Social Security board of trustees has estimated that it would take a tax hike of at least 6.3 percentage points to put the program in the black. A tax hike of that size would force workers to pay one-fifth of their wages to Social Security. Of course, cutting benefits is no solution either; benefit cuts would give workers an even worse deal than does the current system. Many of today's young workers can expect to get a *negative* rate of return from Social Security, according to the nonpartisan Tax Foundation. And, as the American Association of Retired Persons has pointed out, women would suffer most under reform proposals that reduce retiree benefits.

## Benefits of Full Privatization

Women, like men, want to know what would be the likely results under a private system in which payroll tax payments were redirected into personal accounts similar to individual retirement accounts or 401(k) plans. Would private accounts increase the overall level of women's retirement benefits? Would private accounts address poverty among widows? Would private accounts end discrimination against working wives?

To answer those questions, Ekaterina Shirley and Peter Spiegler, graduates of Harvard University's Kennedy School of Government, conducted two empirical analyses. The first is a retrospective analysis using actual earnings histories of 1,585 men and 1,992 women who retired in 1981. The researchers compared Social Security benefits with the benefits that hypothetically would have accrued under a private plan with a 7 percent contribution rate, a 6.2 percent rate of return, and 50-50 earnings sharing between spouses where applicable. Earnings sharing lets married couples split their contributions 50-50 before depositing them into each person's account.

Shirley and Spiegler found that all but .11 percent (approximately 3) of the women collecting benefits would have been better off under the private system. For those women, the difference between the plans was exactly zero—no woman was worse off under the private system. For 3.7 percent (approximately 110) of the women, the difference was less than $2,000. Even though the absolute dollar difference appears small, it is significant relative to total benefits from Social Security. Overall, the median value of the accrued difference between benefits from Social Security and benefits from a privatized plan was $30,000 for single women, $26,000 for wives, $21,000 for divorcees, $23,000 for surviving divorcees, and $20,000 for widows. As a percentage of Social Security benefits, that difference is substantial. The median values of that percentage are 58 percent for single women, 208 percent for wives, 67 percent for divorcees, 58 percent for surviving divorcees, and 97 percent for widows.

In the second analysis, Shirley and Spiegler conducted a prospective simulation since the cohort of women in the workforce today has significantly different labor and marital characteristics than the one that retired in 1981. As complete lifetime earnings histories for women who are currently in the workforce do not exist, the research team simulated the effects of various retirement plans. They compared Social Security; a fully private system; and a two-tiered, or partly private, system. Under the fully private system, the assumed contribution rate is 10 percent. The partly private approach would channel 5 percentage points of payroll taxes into a personal account, with the remaining 7.4 percentage points going to Social Security to finance a "flat benefit" and survivor's and disability insurance. The flat benefit is equal to 2/3 of the poverty rate. As they did in the retrospective analysis, the researchers assumed a 6.2 percent rate of return on invested contributions. . . .

In every case the fully private system with a contribution rate of 10 percent would bring all women—whether collecting benefits based on their own earnings or as wives, divorcees, or widows—with full earnings histories more than twice the retirement benefits of Social Security.

Moreover, the greater the contribution rate, the greater a woman's financial security in retirement. Thus, the fully private system generates significantly higher retirement benefits than does the partly private, two-tiered system. The partly private system provides only slightly greater benefits than Social Security. The results are similar for women who have moved in and out of the job market.

In every case, the fully private system brings all women significantly greater benefits than does either Social Security or the partly private system. For example, the fully private plan gives married, divorced, and widowed women (with full or interrupted earnings histories) at least $200,000 more in retirement benefits than does Social Security or the partly private system. That's better than $10,000 per year.

| *"Many existing benefits important to
women would not be available under
privatization."*

# Privatization of Social Security
# Harms Women

National Organization for Women

Replacing Social Security with individual investments would
pose a significant financial threat to women, the National
Organization for Women (NOW) argues in the following
viewpoint. It contends that older women would be particularly at risk because they are more likely than men to live in
poverty. According to NOW, while Social Security ensures
these women receive a steady income, the value of private
investments would fluctuate with the stock market. The organization asserts that Social Security should not be privatized but should instead be reformed to ensure that women
are properly compensated for their work inside and outside
the home. The National Organization for Women seeks legal, political, and social equality for women.

As you read, consider the following questions:

1. According to the National Organization for Women,
   what proportion of Social Security recipients over the
   age of eighty-five are women?
2. How much of its value did the market lose between 1965
   and 1978, as stated by the author?
3. According to the organization, how does the cap on
   social security taxes affect lower-waged workers?

Reprinted, with permission, from the Winter 1999 issue of the *National NOW
Times*, "Viewpoint: Women Most Vulnerable in Social Security Debate," found at
www.now.org/nnt/winter-99/viewpnt.html.

S ocial security was a top issue for voters in [the 1998] election, and politicians emphasized their commitment to "save Social Security." But beyond this poll-driven catchphrase, candidates failed to tell voters what they really had in mind. Now congressional Republicans and President Clinton have declared their intention to seek a deal on Social Security. Women are skeptical about the prospects, as well we should be.

The question before the president and Congress is simple: As we cross the bridge into the 21st century, are we willing to leave seniors—especially older women—behind?

Congress has already turned its back on the working poor by refusing to increase the minimum wage and, with the collusion of the president, pulled public assistance out from under the unemployed poor. Now conservatives in Congress are turning to Social Security, which benefits not only the elderly, but also people with disabilities, widows and orphans. And we have no reason to believe that Social Security will survive a revamp by [Representative Bob] Livingston and [Senator Trent] Lott . . . unless we can educate and mobilize the public.

## It's Not a Crisis; It's a Scam

A chicken-little atmosphere has been created by the millions of Wall Street dollars pushing for privatization of Social Security. (With the system taking in some $1.5 billion a day, the prospect of fees for managing even a fraction of that amount are quite an incentive.) But the threat we face is not an imminent collapse in Social Security funding, but a possible shortfall after 2032. Congress created the Social Security Trust Fund (financed by the excess of current payroll taxes over current payments to beneficiaries, now growing by more than $100 billion a year) to help the system meet the challenge of supporting baby boomers who will begin to retire in 2010. By 2032, if the Trust Fund is drawn down to zero, the system will be purely pay-as-you-go—as it was from the 1940s through the 1960s.

And those projections are based on a cautious economic forecast. The Social Security Trustees project an annual increase in Gross Domestic Product, adjusted for inflation, of only 1.6% from 1997 to 2029. Growth from 1960 to 1974 averaged 4.1%; from 1975 to 1996, it averaged 2.7%. Maintaining current levels of growth would sustain Social Security through the next century without any changes in the program.

Under the cover of a fantasy funding crisis and in the name of reducing government, conservatives want to revise or eliminate Social Security in favor of individual investment. Privatizers want Generation X to join their attacks against Social Security, but young people should beware. Seniors aren't the only ones who benefit from Social Security. Three million children and their sole caretaker parents depend on Social Security's death and disability benefits to survive. Indeed, Social Security's reach is wide; without it, vulnerable people of all ages will suffer.

## Social Security Is a Women's Issue

Women must be particularly wary of proposals to "fix" Social Security. After a lifetime of work, women often find themselves in dire economic straits during what were supposed to be their golden years. Women are a majority of all Social Security recipients, and roughly three out of four of the recipients over 85 are women. Older women are twice as likely as men to live in poverty and to depend on Social Security as their sole support.

Privatization of Social Security would be risky and expensive. (Administrative costs of Social Security are just 1% of benefits, compared to 12 to 14% for private insurers.) Most of the proposals offered would create private accounts by diverting Social Security taxes while cutting benefits and raising the retirement age to make up for lost revenues.

Many existing benefits important to women would not be available under privatization. For instance, Social Security replaces a higher proportion of low-wage workers' income when they retire. Under a private plan, this progressive aspect of Social Security that provides a buffer for the poor, who are disproportionately women, would be lost.

In addition, lifelong benefits under Social Security are especially important to women, who after reaching 65 have a life expectancy of 19.2 years compared to 15.6 for men. And without the protection of cost-of-living adjustments in ben-

## Pro-Women Social Security Reform

[The National Council of Women's Organizations] has developed a checklist for Social Security reform . . . based on the following principles:

• Reduce the number of elderly women living in poverty.

• Continue to help those with lower lifetime earnings, who are disproportionately women.

• Maintain full cost of living adjustments.

• Strengthen benefits for wives, widows, and divorced women.

• Preserve disability and survivor benefits.

• Protect the most disadvantaged workers from across-the-board benefit cuts.

• Ensure that women's guaranteed benefits are not reduced by individual account plans that are subject to the uncertainties of the stock market.

• Address the care giving and labor force experiences of women.

Heidi Hartman, statement before the Senate Democratic Task Force on Social Security, September 13, 1999.

---

efits, even a modest 3% inflation rate would mean cuts in the purchasing power of a $100 benefit to $74 over 10 years and to $55 after 20 years. Inflation-adjusted private annuities are non-existent in this country, and lifetime annuities, if available, would be prohibitively expensive. What are older women supposed to do if they exhaust their assets before death? And as the economy fluctuates, so will the yields of privatized plans. Between 1965 and 1978 the market lost 45% of its value. Seniors need a steady income they can count on, not the booms and falls of the market. The impact on women would be disastrous.

## Take Action

We must guard against changes that will further impoverish women and use this opportunity to strengthen and make Social Security more equitable. While Social Security is an important program to seniors, the disabled and children who survive the death of a parent, there is a lot of room for improvement. Gender neutral language does not mean equality; 63% of women on Social Security receive benefits based on their husband's earnings (wives' or widows' benefits), while only 1.2% of men receive benefits based on their wife's earnings; 37% of these women had no earnings history and 26% had a higher benefit as a wife or widow than as an earner. Women currently receive an average of only $621 in monthly benefits, while men receive $810.

We challenge Congress and the president to change the distribution of spousal and primary earner benefits to make them equitable so that homemakers are no longer penalized for choosing to work in the home instead of the paid workforce. We want the cap on social security taxes raised; highly compensated workers pay no Social Security on earnings over $68,300 which means low-waged workers carry an extra tax burden that represents a higher rate of total earnings. And we want to establish earnings sharing that will allocate 50% of both spouses' combined earnings to each individual spouse, at long last allowing each spouse to have benefits in her or his own right. In other words, we want women's work—in and out of the home—to be counted and compensated.

We must bring higher visibility and organizing on these issues. Our grassroots activists can and will refocus this debate, insist that politicians level with the public about their plans for Social Security and the impact on the lives of women and our families, and stir and direct public fear and frustration toward effective action.

# Periodical Bibliography

The following articles have been selected to supplement the diverse views presented in this chapter. Addresses are provided for periodicals not indexed in the *Readers' Guide to Periodical Literature*, the *Alternative Press Index*, the *Social Sciences Index*, or the *Index to Legal Periodicals and Books*.

| | |
|---|---|
| John Attarian | "Aging America's Fiscal Nightmare," *World & I*, November 1996. Available from 3600 New York Ave. NE, Washington, DC 20002. |
| Dean Baker | "The Privateers' Free Lunch," *American Prospect*, May/June 1997. |
| Fred Brock | "Save Social Security? From What?" *New York Times*, November 1, 1998. |
| Richard B. Du Boff and John Miller | "Myths and Facts About Privatizing Social Security," *Dollars and Sense*, May/June 1999. |
| Martin Feldstein | "Let's Really Save Social Security," *Wall Street Journal*, February 10, 1998. |
| Ellen Frank | "Rethinking Social Security Reform," *Dissent*, Fall 1999. |
| Kevin Hassett and Glenn Hubbard | "If Alan Greenspan Had Bitten the Bullet . . ." *American Enterprise*, November/December 1999. Available from 1150 17th St. NW, Washington, DC 20036. |
| Laurence J. Kotlikoff | "Privatizing Social Security the Right Way," *Independent Review*, Summer 2000. Available from the Independent Institute, 100 Swan Way, Oakland, CA 94621-1428. |
| Hayden Perry | "Social Security Under Attack," *Against the Current*, September/October 1998. |
| Martha Phillips | "To Save Social Security, Americans Will Have to Work a Little Longer," *Insight on the News*, March 8, 1999. Available from 3600 New York Ave. NE, Washington, DC 20002. |
| David E. Rosenbaum | "Saving Social Security: Comparing Three Plans," *New York Times*, March 24, 1999. |
| Amity Shlaes | "Privatize Social Security? Not Like This." *Wall Street Journal*, December 7, 1998. |
| Tadd Wilson | "Government-Mandated Insecurity," *Freeman*, April 1997. Available from the Foundation for Economic Education, Irvington-on-Hudson, NY 10533. |
| Diana Zuckerman | "The Derailing of Social Security," *Extra*, May/June 1999. |

# CHAPTER 4

# Are Improvements Needed in Elderly Health Care?

# Chapter Preface

Living alone can be difficult for many senior citizens who find previously simple tasks, such as mowing the lawn or preparing meals, no longer easy to accomplish. For the elderly who have lost most of their physical (and sometimes mental) ability, nursing homes are a common option. However, for those who are generally healthy but no longer able or willing to live alone, assisted-living facilities have gained in popularity. These facilities typically feature apartments with common dining rooms, 24-hour emergency care, and assistance with tasks such as getting dressed in the morning or going into town for errands.

As of 1999, 2.2 million elderly Americans lived in assisted-living complexes. These facilities are often praised for the independence they provide their residents. John Greenwald writes in *Time:* "Assisted living gives the elderly some measure of independence, a chance to socialize and needed privacy." For many aging Americans, these complexes offer a welcome alternative to the sometimes stifling atmosphere of nursing homes.

While assisted-living facilities can be ideal for some elderly people, various analysts have noted flaws in their operation. Among the criticisms are that the complexes are often too pricey and are unable to provide adequate care for their residents as they age and become more feeble. In addition, there are no uniform standards, so the quality of care and services provided can vary widely from state to state. Rosalie A. Kane, writing for *Aging Today* magazine, asserts: "The nub of the problem is that apartment-style assisted living serves as both a private residence, with tenants who should expect the privileges of home rental, and a care setting which houses vulnerable people and is therefore appropriate for externally imposed standards." However, Kane contends that it is too early to develop a federal standard and that care should be taken to ensure that regulations do not make assisted living too costly or too much a carbon copy of nursing homes.

Assisted-living facilities are one facet of health care for the elderly, which is the topic of the following chapter.

1

> "Unless it is substantially reformed, the
> existing Medicare bureaucracy threatens
> the quality of health care for . . . millions of
> Americans."

# Medicare Needs Radical Reform

Sandra Mahkorn

Medicare—a federal program established in 1965 to provide health insurance to persons age sixty-five and over—is rife with problems and in need of radical reform, Sandra Mahkorn asserts in the following viewpoint. She contends that Medicare is a huge and overly bureaucratic system that impedes quality care by establishing arbitrary standards that make it difficult for doctors to provide necessary treatments. According to Mahkorn, Medicare cannot be fixed through additional bureaucracy and instead should be replaced with a system that is based on patient choice and market competition. Mahkorn is a visiting fellow in health policy at the Heritage Foundation, a research institute that promotes policies based on the principles of limited government and individual freedom.

As you read, consider the following questions:
1. How many Americans are covered by Medicare, according to the author?
2. According to Mahkorn, why is the Health Care Financing Administration "not a user-friendly institution"?
3. What are the consequences of the prospective payment methodology, in the author's opinion?

Excerpted from Sandra Mahkorn, "Why an Unreformed Medicare System Is Hazardous to Your Health," *Heritage Foundation Backgrounder*, no. 1295, June 18, 1999. Reprinted by permission of The Heritage Foundation.

Too many Medicare patients are unaware that the quality of their health care is in jeopardy. The almost 40 million older adults and disabled persons who are covered by Medicare are subject to the most aggressively managed and overregulated health plan in the United States. In fact, the federal health care regulations, rulings, and paperwork pertaining to Medicare consume over 111,000 pages, many times more than even the federal income tax code. The complexity of the Medicare system makes it difficult for both patients and their health care providers to understand what procedures and treatments will be covered, and which ones will be ruled medically unnecessary.

Members of Congress determine in legislation what can be covered under Medicare and at what price. They avoid making the tough decisions affecting patients, however, by shifting responsibility for Medicare coverage to the Health Care Financing Administration (HCFA). HCFA, in turn, regulates the delivery of health care by imposing voluminous rules, regulations, and guidelines on doctors, hospitals, and other health care providers. But it is a profound mistake to think that Medicare patients are insulated from the negative effects of this huge regulatory system in Washington by their physicians and providers. Their treatment is often at the mercy of distant federal bureaucrats and Medicare contractors.

## Medicare Prevents Quality Care

If Members of Congress want to find ways to improve health care for all Americans, they should examine the many roadblocks to quality care that Medicare imposes on those who provide health care to senior citizens and disabled Americans. For example:

• *Medicare's standards for determining "medical necessity" are arbitrary and ill-defined.* Curiously, Members of Congress are considering private-sector health care legislation that would shift the responsibility of determining medical necessity to physicians, not bureaucrats.

• *Doctors who treat Medicare patients face the dilemma of choosing treatments based on their best professional judgment, and risking fraud and abuse charges if the Medicare bureaucracy says the treatments are "unnecessary," or if it proscribes the treatments.*

This *Catch-22* undermines the professional independence of physicians and imposes a de facto gag rule.

• *The many complicated Medicare provider payment schemes include perverse incentives that interfere with the provision of medical services.* The complex "resource-based relative value scale" (RBRVS), for example, is a method of determining physician payment based on a statistical calculation of the "value" of factors that go into a medical service, outside the normal forces of supply and demand or patient benefit.

• *Patients who challenge Medicare denials of their claims face an arduous review and appeals process. HCFA concedes that, in 1998, the average processing time for appeals of claims denied under Medicare Part A, which pays for hospital services, was 310 days.* For Medicare Part B claims, which covers physicians' services, the average time for administrative law judges to render a decision was 524 days.

• *Even if an appeal is decided in their favor, Medicare beneficiaries can hope to recover only the cost of the benefit itself, regardless of the extent of injury that resulted from the claim's original denial.* Yet in the context of private health plans, Senator Edward M. Kennedy (D-Massachusetts) has declared, "Health plans should not be allowed to escape responsibility for their actions when their decisions kill or injure patients."

HCFA is not a user-friendly institution. Medicare policies and procedures stand as a regulatory gate between patients and quality care, with HCFA bureaucrats and HCFA contractors functioning as gatekeepers. Patients and doctors are poorly informed about issues as basic as the services that are covered and the financial disincentives doctors and hospitals face. Almost 24 percent of all physician and supplier claims were denied in 1997. Even excluding those denied for "reason of statutory exclusion," the rate of Medicare carrier denial is more than 1 in 10 claims. And patients or doctors who can afford the inordinate time and energy involved in filing appeals of denied claims recoup only the cost of the service or benefit.

Although Members of Congress and HCFA officials routinely give lip service to quality, practical experience with the Medicare program tells a different story. Today's problems with Medicare are minor compared with what they are likely to become with the retirement of the 77 million-strong baby-boom generation and the corresponding demand for medical services. Shortsighted reimbursement and coverage decisions, poor communication with doctors, and intimidation of providers combine with intermittent managerial crises, invasion of patient privacy, and restrictions on patients' liberty to make the program a national concern. More than three decades' worth of circuitous and contradictory policies confuses doctors and patients alike. And Medicare has no competition to force it to improve. If Medicare beneficiaries want alternative health insurance coverage for their physicians' services, for all practical purposes they are stuck, for better or for worse.

In early 1999, 10 of the 17 members of the National Bipartisan Commission on the Future of Medicare, chaired by Senator John Breaux (D-Louisiana) and Representative Bill Thomas (R-California), endorsed a serious proposal that would reform Medicare substantially. That proposal would give Medicare beneficiaries roughly the same types of choices enjoyed by millions of government workers and retirees in the Federal Employees Health Benefits Program (FEHBP).

If Congress is serious about improving America's troubled health care system, it should offer expanded personal choice to all Americans, regardless of whether they are enrolled in a federal plan, private plans, or the Medicare program. In the private sector, expanded choice should be accompanied by personal selection and ownership of health plans, and portability of benefits when workers change jobs. In Medicare, it would mean that patients could keep the traditional plan if they wanted to do so, but it also would mean that they could pick and choose superior private plans or bring their private health plan with them into retirement for primary coverage and get a government contribution to offset its cost.

## A Financially Troubled System

Medicare originally was designed in 1965 as a program to provide health insurance for the elderly. It since has evolved into a huge, financially troubled, overly bureaucratic system of rules and regulations governing virtually every facet of financing and delivering medical services to senior citizens and disabled patients. Medicare's tight control of benefits and providers is secure, with its burgeoning regulatory morass and unintelligible payment schemes.

Medicare is administered by the powerful Health Care Financing Administration. The regulatory history of HCFA has been a series of failed attempts to control and manage all aspects of medical practice, from the numbers and types of providers and the frequency of treatments and tests to the rates of reimbursement. Medicare's missteps have resulted in new layers of regulations to "correct" the unintended consequences of prior attempts. In study after study, the U.S. General Accounting Office (GAO) finds that Medicare frequently pays providers too much or too little.

---

## A Terminally Ill System

Medicare is terminally ill. As recently as 1997, its trustees calculated that the mandatory part of Medicare (Part A) would deplete its trust fund by the year 2001. Congressional fiddling and our recent stellar economic growth have now postponed the day of reckoning to more like 2008 or so. But don't count on much more of a reprieve.

Now is the time for everyone concerned about burdensome taxes and the continued growth of the welfare state to focus like a laser on federal health entitlements. If these can be reformed, Americans can be spared massive future tax hikes and weaned off of government dependency. If not, then the 60-year war waged by advocates of limited government against the New Deal and the Great Society will be irretrievably lost.

John Hood, *American Enterprise*, July/August 1999.

---

Testifying before the National Bipartisan Commission on the Future of Medicare, Dr. Robert Waller, President of the Mayo Foundation, pointed out that federal health care regulations consume over 132,000 pages. The vast majority of these rules, regulations, and related paperwork—more than 111,000 pages—pertain to Medicare. Between 1994 and 1998, 30,000 more pages were published in the *Federal Register*, compared with 2,000 the previous four years. This explosion of health care regulation is occurring despite White House promises in 1995 to simplify the regulations governing Medicare. The ever-growing pile of Medicare paperwork dwarfs that of any other government agency, including the Internal Revenue Service (IRS), which accounts for 17,000 pages of laws and regulations in the tax code. As a result, Medicare rules are becoming increasingly unintelligible to doctors and patients alike.

HCFA's regulatory regime is far more aggressive and intrusive than ever before. The Medicare bureaucracy has gone so far as to extend its regulatory reach into private transactions taking place *outside* the confines of the Medicare program, such as its private contract agreements between doctors and patients in which no taxpayer dollars are involved. Even worse, HCFA now proposes to collect detailed and sensitive personal information from Medicare patients served by home health care agencies and transmitting it to a huge federal data base without the knowledge of the patients.

## Micromanaging Treatment

Federal and state legislators often chide private insurance plans for payment or reimbursement schemes that appear to reward doctors for withholding expensive tests or treatments. For example, in some managed care plans, a portion of "capitation" allotments are "withheld" until the end of the provider's contract year. Payment of these withholdings is contingent on the managed care plan's achieving certain medical spending targets. Curiously, Congress has allowed HCFA to utilize financial and punitive disincentives for expensive care and treatments for more years than most managed care plans have been in existence.

HCFA's Prospective Payment System is a case in point. Hospitals are paid a set amount on the basis of a patient's final diagnosis at the time of discharge instead of the actual number of services, tests, and treatments the patient may require. For example, HCFA reimburses a hospital more generously for the inpatient costs to treat one type of pneumonia over another, even when the patient with the lower-cost pneumonia may require more care and services and longer hospitalization.

The prospective payment methodology for hospitals encourages strict, sometimes draconian, utilization reviews for sick, hospitalized patients. It is not uncommon for admitting physicians to order unnecessary intravenous lines or urinary catheterizations—placing the patient at unnecessary risk for such problems as phlebitis [inflammation of the leg veins] or urinary tract infections—to prevent the patient from being discharged when they believe it is not in the patient's best medical interest. The reason: Hospitals have an economic incentive to "evict" patients as quickly as possible to avoid financial loss or to maximize monetary gain.

HCFA is notorious for developing elaborate payment schemes to influence the care-giving behavior of physicians and other providers by using a series of rewards, punishments, and even threats of punishment. It is doubtful that private-sector managed care plans, faced with even minimal free-market competition, could have imposed most of HCFA's highly aggressive cost-containment measures without hearing a resounding public and political outcry. Medicare's large and growing captive membership provides effective immunity from the consumer pressures regularly experienced by private-sector plans. There is no existing private insurance market for seniors outside Medicare, a fact admitted by the Clinton Administration's counsel in recent litigation over the rights of Medicare patients. Today, American seniors have no real alternative to Medicare for private coverage. The lack of real choice for Medicare beneficiaries makes congressional attentiveness to a patient's right to quality care in Medicare even more important. . . .

## Reform Is Essential

Unless it is substantially reformed, the existing Medicare bureaucracy threatens the quality of health care for the growing millions of Americans who depend on Medicare for their primary coverage. Medicare patients and doctors alike are ill-informed about what really is covered. Bureaucratic doublespeak results in arbitrary payment denials. Expanded definitions of fraud and abuse and circuitous definitions of "medical necessity" create a *Catch-22* situation for doctors and result in a de facto gag rule. The many Medicare contractors and professional review organizations that are supposed to promote care quality have become bounty hunters. Few Medicare patients know or understand what really is going on within the program. And worse, those who want better treatment have no real choices.

The real fix for Medicare is not more rules and regulations, another insufferable pile of paperwork, some palliative treatment, or tinkering at the edges. Radical surgery of the program's heavy bureaucratic control is needed. The best approach to the problem of patient care in both the private and public sectors is the expansion of patient choice, which would enable individuals and families to pick the kinds of plans and benefits they personally want and need. The National Bipartisan Commission on the Future of Medicare came close to a formal recommendation of expanding choice when the majority of its members supported a model for reform that is similar to the consumer-driven system enjoyed by federal employees, Members of Congress, and White House staff— the Federal Employees Health Benefits Program.

Real Medicare reform is medically necessary, and it should put patients first. Members of Congress should create a new and better system based on patient choice and market competition, one that respects the personal liberty and privacy of Medicare patients as well as the medical expertise of their physicians.

VIEWPOINT

*2*

*"It is essential that policy makers and the public understand proposed changes to Medicare and their effect on beneficiaries, providers, and the Medicare program."*

# Medicare Should Be Reformed Cautiously

Tess Canja

In the following viewpoint, excerpted from testimony before Congress, Tess Canja argues that while Medicare is in need of reform, such reform should be done cautiously so as to ensure the continued success of the program. Canja contends any reform should build on the foundation that was created by the Medicare+Choice program. According to Canja, such reform must be done carefully in order to ensure that policy makers and the public understand the effects of any changes. Canja is the president of the AARP (formerly the American Association of Retired Persons), a nonpartisan association that is dedicated to improving the experience of aging for all Americans.

As you read, consider the following questions:

1. What was the impact of the Balanced Budget Act on Medicare, as explained by Canja?
2. In the author's view, what are some of the problems caused by private sector solutions to Medicare's problems?
3. According to Canja, what percentage of his or her income does the average Medicare beneficiary spend on out-of-pocket health care expenses?

Excerpted from Tess Canja's testimony before U.S. House of Representatives Committee on Commerce, Subcommittee on Health and the Environment, August 4, 1999.

Good morning Mr. Chairman and members of the Committee. I am Tess Canja, President-elect of AARP. Thank you for this opportunity to share with you the beneficiary perspective on the Medicare+Choice program and the future of Medicare.

## The Importance of Medicare

While this hearing is focused on evaluating the Medicare+ Choice program and addressing its strengths and weaknesses, let me start by underscoring the enormous importance of Medicare. For over thirty years Medicare has provided dependable, affordable, quality health insurance for millions of older and disabled Americans. My home state of Florida has one of the largest beneficiary populations in the nation, and I see firsthand what a difference Medicare makes in the lives of older Americans. Medicare has been instrumental in improving the health and life expectancy of beneficiaries in Florida and across the nation. It has also helped to reduce the number of older persons living in poverty.

Medicare's promise of affordable health care extends beyond the current generation of retirees. Now, more than ever, Americans of all ages are looking to Medicare's guaranteed protections as part of the foundation of their retirement planning. AARP believes that in order for Medicare to remain strong and viable for beneficiaries today and in the future, we must confront the key challenges facing the program. Among these challenges are: keeping pace with advances in medicine and changes in health care delivery; and securing the necessary long-term financial stability for the program in light of the aging of the boomer generation.

To control the growth in Medicare expenditures and offer beneficiaries more health plan options, in 1997 Congress passed, and AARP supported, the Balanced Budget Act (BBA). The BBA provided significant program savings that extended Medicare's solvency until 2008; the recent report of the Medicare Trustees projected 7 additional years of solvency—to 2015. At the same time, the BBA addressed a number of problems with the Medicare managed care program. It modified the payment methodology for plans to address significant overpayment problems. It also made several major changes affecting the program's beneficiaries, including: the creation of the Medicare+Choice program through which new types of plans could participate in Medicare; formulation of new rules for when and how beneficiaries can enroll in health plans or Medigap plans; and requirements specifying the content of information beneficiaries receive about those choices. In addition, as a result of the changes mandated by the BBA, virtually every beneficiary will face higher out-of-pocket expenses for health care.

AARP supported the BBA and its creation of Medicare+Choice in order to accomplish the objective of expanding choice in the program while also protecting access, affordability, and quality of health care services. We understood that extending the short term solvency of the Medicare program required shared sacrifice from all who have a stake in Medicare, including both providers and beneficiaries. We also recognized that Medicare+Choice would lay the foundation for essential longer term reform in the Medicare program.

## Lessons Learned from Medicare+Choice

The challenges and successes of Medicare+Choice will have important implications for the next phase of Medicare reform. The initial implementation of Medicare+Choice offers several valuable lessons:

• First, the significant withdrawals from the program by Medicare HMOs both in 1999 and 2000 serve as a wake-up call to all who seek to bring private sector solutions to bear on Medicare's problems. While some private managed care approaches have been able to help remedy some glaring gaps in original Medicare—namely, the lack of prescription drug coverage and high out-of-pocket costs—these are not without their own failings. When private businesses are given the authority to manage a beneficiary's care in exchange for the opportunity to earn a profit, several things can happen. On the positive side, the innovations in administrative efficiency and improved health care delivery may benefit the patient through lower costs, additional benefits, and better coordinated care. On the other hand, patients can be exposed to the vagaries of the market place. They may face instability in their benefits and premium charges, and worse yet, benefi-

139

ciaries may not know from one year to the next whether their plan will remain a Medicare option. It is a challenge to separate the positive from the negative because the same factors create both results. A private business may be more innovative and efficient, yet in the absence of an opportunity to earn a profit, will leave (or not enter) the market. This dynamic is part of the market place—particularly for publicly traded companies who have a responsibility to their investors. The beneficiary who gained extra benefits in the short run may lose them in the long run. Congress anticipated this problem and provided some protections for beneficiaries who move back into original fee-for-service Medicare.

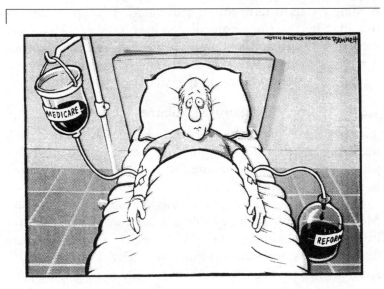

Clay Bennett/North America Syndicate. Reprinted with permission.

• Second, with every change to Medicare, there are unintended consequences. Therefore, it is essential that policy makers and the public understand proposed changes to Medicare and their effect on beneficiaries, providers, and the Medicare program. This is especially important as Congress moves forward on additional Medicare changes. There must be a careful and thorough examination of the full range of issues, including how the issues interact, as well as an understanding of the trade-offs that will be necessary.

The [Senator John] Breaux-[Representative Bill] Thomas premium support plan and the President's [July 1999] Medicare reform proposal provide opportunities for examining different reform options and for stimulating public debate. Genuine debate is critical to build public understanding and support for reform. AARP believes it would be a serious mistake for anyone to hinder debate or for Congress to rush to judgment on any reform option. *However, if reform legislation is pushed through too quickly, before the effects on beneficiaries and the program are known and before there is an emerging public judgment, AARP would be compelled to alert our members of the dangers of such legislation and why we would oppose it.*

• Third, the significant number of Medicare HMO withdrawals has highlighted the difficulties older Americans have because outpatient prescription drugs are not included in Medicare's benefit package. Beneficiaries who seek drug coverage may find Medicare HMOs are not available in many locations. Those who do enroll in Medicare HMOs for drug coverage are finding that drug benefits are becoming more expensive and/or more restrictive, or that they may lose the benefit or the option of enrolling in an HMO altogether due to plan withdrawals. Once these beneficiaries return to original fee-for-service Medicare, it is almost impossible for them to purchase a supplemental policy that includes some prescription drug coverage due to cost and medical underwriting.

• Fourth, beneficiary education about their Medicare options is critical to the success of the Medicare+Choice program. AARP supported Medicare+Choice in order to give beneficiaries the full benefit of innovations in health care delivery. However, Medicare+Choice can realize its potential only if beneficiaries acquire the knowledge that will enable them to exercise their leverage as informed consumers in the health care market place. We support the Health Care Financing Administration's (HCFA) efforts to educate beneficiaries, and AARP has joined with the Agency as a partner in its education efforts. We believe Congress, too, must do its part by providing sufficient resources to enable HCFA to carry out its challenging tasks. In addition, we believe it is important that Congress not be overly prescriptive in defining HCFA's education initiatives, but rather allow HCFA the flexibility to employ a range of education techniques and materials for beneficiaries. . . .

## Key Principles for Medicare Reform

As we have noted, Medicare+Choice is still in its infancy and many of the changes enacted by the Balanced Budget Act are still phasing in. The overall effects of these changes on beneficiaries, providers, and the Medicare program itself are not yet clear and there is much to be learned. The challenges and the successes of Medicare+Choice will have important implications for broader reform of the Medicare program. The amount of "fine-tuning" now under discussion for Medicare+Choice offers ample reason why larger-scale reforms in Medicare must be made slowly and cautiously.

While we have stated the importance of understanding the impact of the changes that have already been made before new changes are layered on top, this does not mean that the status quo in Medicare is acceptable. More must be done to ensure the program's long-term solvency and to modernize Medicare's benefits and delivery system.

To this end, AARP believes that the fundamental principles that have guided Medicare should continue to be the basis of any efforts to reform the program:

• *Defined Benefits Including Prescription Drugs*—All Medicare beneficiaries are now guaranteed a defined set of health care benefits upon which they depend. A specified benefit package that is set in statute assures that Medicare remains a dependable source of health coverage over time. It is also an important benchmark upon which the adequacy of the government's contribution toward the cost of care can be measured. A benefit package set in statute reduces the potential for adverse selection by providing an appropriate basis for competition among the health plans participating in Medicare, and provides an element of certainty around which individuals, employers, and state Medicaid programs may plan.

When Medicare began, the benefit package was consistent with the standards for medical care at the time. In any reform, it will be important that the benefits be clearly defined and reflect modern medical practices. To this end, prescription drugs must become part of the standard Medicare benefit package and can be available to all beneficiaries in whatever plan they choose.

• *Adequate Government Contribution Toward the Cost of the Benefit Package*—It is essential that the government's contribution or payment for the Medicare benefit package keep pace over time with the cost of the benefits. Currently, payment for traditional Medicare is roughly tied to the cost of the benefit package. If the government's contribution were tied to an artificial budget target and not connected to the benefit package, there would be a serious risk that both the benefits and government payment would diminish over time. In addition, a change that results in a flat government payment—regardless of the cost of a plan premium—could yield sharp out-of-pocket premium differences, both year-to-year and among plans, with resulting volatility in enrollments.

• *Out-of-Pocket Protection*—Changes in Medicare financing and benefits should protect all beneficiaries from burdensome out-of-pocket costs. The average Medicare beneficiary spends nearly 20 percent of his or her income out-of-pocket for health care expenses, excluding the costs of long-term care. In addition to items and services not covered by Medicare, beneficiaries have significant Medicare cost-sharing obligations: a $100 annual Part B deductible, a $768 Part A hospital deductible, 20 percent coinsurance for most Part B services, a substantially higher coinsurance for hospital outpatient services and mental health care, and a significant coinsurance for skilled nursing facility care. Currently, there is no coinsurance for Medicare home health care.

Beneficiaries already pay a substantial amount of their health care costs—from services not covered by Medicare, to Medicare's cost-sharing obligations, to their $45.50 monthly Part B premium. Further, the Part B premium beneficiaries pay is expected to almost double in the next ten years.

AARP believes that beneficiaries are now paying, and should continue to pay their fair share for Medicare. However, if their cost-sharing became too high, Medicare beneficiaries would face increasingly unaffordable barriers to appropriate and necessary services. In addition, if cost-sharing varies too greatly across plans, the potential for greater risk selection would increase, leaving many beneficiaries with coverage options they might consider inadequate or unsatisfactory.

## Protect Medicare

• *Protecting the Availability and Affordability of Medicare Coverage*—Medicare should continue to be available to all older and disabled Americans regardless of their health status or income. Our nation's commitment to a system in which Americans contribute to the program through payroll taxes during their working years and then are entitled to receive the benefits they have earned, is the linchpin of public support for Medicare. Denying Medicare coverage to individuals based on income threatens this support. Furthermore, raising the age of Medicare eligibility would have the likely effect of leaving more Americans uninsured. Thus, in the absence of changes that would protect access to affordable coverage, raising the eligibility age for Medicare is unacceptable to AARP.

• *Administration of Medicare*—Effective administration of the program remains essential. The agency or organization that oversees Medicare must be accountable to Congress and beneficiaries for assuring access, affordability, adequacy of coverage, quality of care, and choice. It must have the tools and the flexibility it needs to improve the program—such as the ability to try new options like competitive bidding or expanding centers of excellence. It must ensure that a level playing field exists across all options; modernize original Medicare fee-for-service so that it remains a viable option for beneficiaries; ensure that all health plans meet rigorous standards; and continue to rigorously attack waste, fraud and abuse in the program.

• *Financing*—Medicare must have a stable source of financing that keeps pace with enrollment and the costs of the program. Ultimately, any financing source will need to be both broadly based and progressive. Additionally, AARP supports using an appropriate portion of the on-budget surplus to ensure Medicare's financial health beyond 2015.

The initial implementation of Medicare+Choice is teaching us some valuable lessons. It is essential that changes from the BBA and their impact on current and future beneficiaries are thoroughly analyzed before greater changes take place. AARP looks forward to continuing to work with the Commerce Committee and your colleagues in the House and Senate to improve upon the Medicare+Choice program. We also want to work with you to advance a Medicare reform package that includes prescription drug coverage. The status quo in Medicare is not acceptable, but together we must ensure that any reform package continues Medicare's promise of quality, affordable health care.

> "*A typical senior without prescription drug coverage pays 34% of their after-tax income on health care.*"

# Medicare Should Provide Prescription Drug Coverage

Gail Shearer

The current Medicare program does not cover prescription drugs. In the following viewpoint, Gail Shearer provides ten reasons why Medicare should be reformed to provide such coverage. She claims that seniors who lack prescription drug coverage spend a significant percentage of their income on their prescriptions. According to Shearer, these seniors also pay higher prices for these drugs than seniors with private health insurance coverage. She contends that Medicare should establish a prescription drug benefit that limits out-of-pocket costs. Shearer is the director of health policy analysis for Consumers Union. Consumers Union, a nonprofit organization that provides information on consumer concerns.

As you read, consider the following questions:

1. According to Shearer, what percentage of people aged sixty-five years and older spend more than 10 percent of their income on out-of-pocket health care costs?
2. Why is prescription drug spending for the elderly predictable, as stated by the author?
3. According to the author, what happened when the New Hampshire Medicaid program limited its beneficiaries to three prescriptions per month?

Excerpted from Gail Shearer, "Prescription Drugs for Medicare Beneficiaries: Ten Important Facts," April 14, 1999, web article found at www.consumersunion.org/health/drugdc400.htm. Reprinted by permission of the author.

The debate about a prescription drug benefit for Medicare beneficiaries is intensifying. Members of Congress from both sides of the aisle have put forward proposals. As the months go by, the out-of-pocket costs for prescription drugs paid by Medicare beneficiaries (those 65 and over and people under 65 who qualify for Medicare due to a disability) pose a growing financial burden. Health policy journals are focusing on the topic. On April 10, 2000, the Clinton Administration released a new Department of Health and Human Services report. This viewpoint presents some of the most important data and facts that policymakers need to have to shape a Medicare prescription drug benefit that is effective in reducing financial burdens on Medicare beneficiaries who need prescription drugs. . . .

## Prescription Drugs Are Costly

1. Out-of-pocket prescription drug costs impose a large financial burden on Medicare beneficiaries.

• A typical senior without prescription drug coverage pays 34% of their after-tax income on health care.

• Even people with good prescription drug coverage can face large out-of-pocket costs for their medications.

• Out-of-pocket drug spending is significantly higher for those without drug coverage than for those with drug coverage (on average $463 in 1996 for those without coverage, vs. $253 for those with coverage). Researchers concluded that those without drug coverage are "underserved in receiving drug therapies."

• In large part because of prescription drug expenditures, 57 percent of people 65 and over have out-of-pocket health care costs greater than 10 percent of their income.

• AARP research found that prescription drugs spending is the single largest component of out-of-pocket spending on health care (other than premium payments). "On average, beneficiaries are expected to spend as much out-of-pocket for prescription drugs as for physician care, vision services, and medical supplies combined."

2. Prescription drugs, which have never been covered by Medicare, are an increasingly important part of the health care needs of Medicare beneficiaries.

• New drugs can replace surgery (e.g., heart bypass surgery), help prevent brain damage in people who have strokes, lower cholesterol levels, and provide relief for chronic pain.

• According to the AARP, 80 percent of retirees use a prescription drug every day. Older Americans account for one-third of prescription drug spending, though they represent just 12 percent of the population.

• The number of prescriptions used by beneficiaries has grown from 16.6 (1992) to 19.5 (1996).

3. The medigap market does not provide high-value (cost-effective) coverage for prescription drugs. [Medigap insurance is private health insurance that fills in some of the gaps not covered by Medicare.]

• Because of the premium structure in most policies (which build in premium increases as a person gets older), older seniors pay very high premiums for policies with prescription drug coverage. For example, an 80-year-old in South Carolina would pay $2,904 for policy I (with a maximum drug benefit of $1,250) vs. $1,863 for a 65-year-old. An 80-year-old would pay $1,683 for policy F (with no drug benefit) in South Carolina. (In other words, the 80-year-old is paying an extra premium that is equivalent to the maximum benefit under the policy.)

• 75-year-olds pay, on average, $1,847 more per year for medigap plan I (with a maximum prescription drug benefit of $1,250) than for medigap Plan C, with nearly comparable benefits except for the absence of prescription drugs.

• In most medigap policies, premiums increase with age, making medigap prescription drug coverage least affordable for the oldest beneficiaries.

• Prescription drug coverage through medigap tends to be unstable: about 48 percent of beneficiaries with medigap drug coverage had such coverage for only part of the year.

## Inadequate Insurance

4. Employer-based coverage of prescription drugs for Medicare beneficiaries often provides comprehensive coverage, but is unavailable for the majority of people.

• 8.6 million Medicare beneficiaries, one-quarter of Medicare beneficiaries, had employer-sponsored supplemental insurance that provided year-round prescription drug protection.

• Only about half of Medicare beneficiaries had any type of drug coverage for the entire year of 1996.

• Employer coverage of retirees is eroding: the General Accounting Office (GAO) reported that the proportion of employers offering health coverage to retirees decreased from 40 percent in 1993 to 28 percent in 1999, and employers shifted more of the premium cost to retirees. Other studies confirm substantial decreases in employer-sponsored retiree coverage.

• Medicare HMO prescription drug coverage is limited; nearly three-quarters of plans cap benefits at or below $1,000. In 15 states, no Medicare managed care basic plans include prescription drugs.

5. Seniors typically pay higher prices for their prescription drugs than do those with health insurance coverage.

• People without drug coverage ("the typical cash customer") paid nearly 15 percent more than the customer with third party coverage in 1999.

• A series of reports by the Minority Staff, Committee on Government Reform, U.S. House of Representatives found price differentials of over 100 percent between senior citizens and drug companies' most favored customers. In other words, seniors pay more than twice the price that insurance companies and government buyers pay for medications needed for cholesterol, ulcers, high blood pressure, heart problems and depression.

• A Families USA study found that prices of the 50 prescription drugs used most often by the elderly increased by more than four times inflation during 1998.

• Five price surveys by Public Citizen (with state-based groups) found price discrimination by pharmaceutical manufacturers: on average, seniors are being charged double the retail price charged by prescription drug makers to their most favored customers.

• According to researchers at the Boston University School of Public Health, Americans paid 32% more than Canadians for the same drugs in the early 1990's, and the differential is probably growing. $16.2 billion could be saved each year if Americans paid the same wholesale prices paid by Canadians.

6. Prescription drug costs are increasing rapidly; out-of-pocket costs will continue to be burdensome unless new policy addresses both coverage and the need for discounts or other mechanisms to curb growing costs.

• While overall health care expenditures grew at 5 percent per year between 1993 and 1998, prescription drug spending grew at an average of 12.4 percent per year from 1993 to 1998, with a growth rate of 15.4 percent in 1998.

• Prescription drugs have increased, as a percent of total health care spending, from 5.6 percent in 1993 to 7.9 percent in 1998.

• U.S. drug prices are rising 2.4 times as fast as the overall Consumer Price Index, at an annual rate of 6.1 percent in early 1999.

• Because of rising prescription drug costs, Public Citizen has estimated that a senior with average drug expenditures will have higher inflation-adjusted out-of-pocket expenditures after the fourth year, if the Clinton plan were adopted.

7. Prescription drug expenditures vary dramatically across the elderly population, making it difficult if not impossible to design a voluntary system that can avoid splitting the risk pool—segmenting the healthy from the sick.

• Prescription drug spending for the elderly is largely predictable (since it is often for chronic conditions), increasing the likelihood that adverse selection will be a major factor in a voluntary system.

• While average prescription drug spending of people 65 and over was $720 in 1996, those in the top decile spent $3,367. (See chart.) In 1996, more than half of people 65 and over spent less than $500 on prescription drugs. Projections from the 1995 Medicare Current Beneficiary Study estimate 1999 average outpatient prescription drug costs to be $942.

• Data from the 1995 Current Medicare Beneficiary Survey for seniors whose prescription benefit was managed by Merck-Medco Managed Care shows a high degree of variation in spending, with mean spending (for people 65 and over with expenditures) $1,343, and spending for those in

# Common Prescriptions

America's top-selling drugs are used heavily by seniors, one of the groups least able to afford them. Sales and ranking data are for January through September 1998.

| DRUG | USAGE | PRICE (one-month supply) | 1997 SALES (billions) | % OF SALES TO SENIORS |
|---|---|---|---|---|
| Prilosec | Anti-ulcer | $116.09, 20 mg | $2.1 | 33% |
| Prozac | Antidepressant | $75.04, 20 mg | 1.7 | 9 |
| Lipitor | Controls cholesterol | $84.60, 20 mg | 1.2 | 38 |
| Zocor | Controls cholesterol | $105.48, 20 mg | 1.2 | 47 |
| Zoloft | Antidepressant | $71.41, 50 mg | 1.1 | 16 |
| Claritin | Anti-allergy medication | $69.57, 10 mg | 1.0 | 12 |
| Paxil | Antidepressant | $71.84, 20 mg | 0.9 | 16 |
| Prevacid | Anti-ulcer drug | $107.83, 30 mg | 0.9 | 28 |
| Norvasc | Controls high blood pressure | $70.23, 10 mg | 0.9 | 49 |
| Augmentin | Antibiotic | $97.34*, 875 mg | 0.7 | 7 |

*10-day therapy

Sources: Scott-Levin, Newtown, Pa.; Upchurch Drugs & Optical Center, Durham, N.C.

the 99th percentile $6,597.

8. Medicare beneficiaries without prescription drug coverage use fewer prescriptions than people with such coverage; coverage affects health.

• Coverage for prescription drugs lowers the chance that people with hypertension will go without needed antihypertensive drugs. Specifically, the Blustein study "found that a one dollar increase in the out-of-pocket per tablet cost resulted in the purchase of 114 fewer tablets per year."

• The Medicare population with prescription drug coverage spent (on average) $769 on prescription drugs, compared with $463 for those without drug coverage. Among the Medicare population with poor health, people with drug coverage spent $1,340 on prescription drugs, vs. $749 for those without drug coverage.

• Analysis of data from the 1996 Medicare Current Beneficiary Survey shows that beneficiaries without supplemental prescription drug coverage had 16.7 prescriptions filled, while those with year-round coverage had 22.4 prescriptions filled.

• Harvard Medical School researchers estimated that

Medicare enrollees whose incomes were less than $10,000 used less than half as many prescription drugs as higher income individuals who had employer drug coverage.

• When the New Hampshire Medicaid program switched from unlimited prescription coverage to 3 prescriptions per month, the use of "essential life-saving drugs like insulin for diabetes, furosemide for congestive heart failure, bronchodilators for asthma, and lithium for bipolar illness, to decline substantially." There were numerous adverse effects of this cutback in medicines.

9. Design of benefits matters: an important tool for relieving financial burden is stop-loss protection.

• "Stop-loss" design would limit beneficiary out-of-pocket prescription drug costs through a benefit design that has Medicare pay all prescription drug costs after the beneficiary has out-of-pocket expenditures exceeding a certain level (e.g., $2,000). "Stop-loss" protection provides catastrophic coverage (in contrast to a design that limits coverage) to a certain level such as $2,500, thus protecting those with the highest prescription drug costs.

• Policy proposals that lack a stop-loss prescription drug coverage (e.g., July 1999 Clinton plan, Breaux-Frist proposal [Senators John Breaux of Louisiana and Bill Frist of Tennessee]), many Medicare beneficiaries, especially those with severe chronic diseases, would continue to face high out-of-pocket drug costs.

10. Cost control mechanisms that are effective in the private marketplace may not work well for the Medicare program.

• Little is known about the effects on costs and quality of care of Medicare prescription drug-use management strategies (such as private pharmacy benefit managers, PBMs).

• Some of the limitations of using PBMs to manage a Medicare drug benefit include: (1) savings can not be ensured if Congress and HCFA do not allow PBMs to use a broad range of techniques to promote the use of cost-effective drugs; (2) potential conflicts of interest (when PBMs use formularies to favor one brand-name drug over another) would be more difficult to resolve in a public program than in the private sector; (3) the public might protest against PBM efforts to promote cost-effective drugs.

# How to Establish a Prescription Drug Benefit

• A new Medicare prescription drug benefit should be universal, just as coverage for hospital care protects all Medicare beneficiaries.

• Financial burdens on low-income Medicare beneficiaries (e.g., those with incomes below 135 percent of poverty) should be alleviated through a full subsidization of any premiums and cost-sharing.

• The benefit should include a "stop-loss" that limits out-of-pocket prescription drug costs to a certain amount, protecting those with the largest expenditures.

• Competition (e.g., large purchase discounts) must be put to work to lower costs of medicines. A new benefit should assure that prices charged by pharmaceutical companies are in line with underlying costs of developing and distributing prescription drugs, and that there be accountability to the public interest.

• The new benefit should be financed fairly and progressively (e.g., with moderate and high-income beneficiaries paying premiums), and with the subsidy for low-income beneficiaries spread broadly across people of all ages.

• "Choice" of a prescription drug benefit (i.e., having a voluntary benefit) should be resisted unless there is a mechanism capable of preventing adverse selection.

> *"We cannot solve the problem of prescription drug coverage for the elderly without addressing the structural problems of Medicare."*

# Medicare Is Not the Best Solution for Prescription Drug Coverage

John C. Goodman and Sean R. Tuffnell

In the following viewpoint, John C. Goodman and Sean R. Tuffnell contend that prescription drug coverage should be provided through a private plan rather than Medicare. They argue that the funds the elderly receive through Medicare should be combined with the money they already spend on supplemental insurance and used to purchase private coverage. Goodman is the president and Tuffnell is the communications manager for the National Center for Policy Analysis, a nonpartisan research institute.

As you read, consider the following questions:

1. According to a 1996 study cited by the authors, for every dollar spent on prescription drugs, how much money is saved in hospital expenses?
2. How much would the average senior save if he or she chose a fee-for-service plan instead of a combination of Medicare and Medigap, as stated by Goodman and Tuffnell?
3. What do the authors think is the biggest obstacle to Medicare reform?

Excerpted from John C. Goodman and Sean R. Tuffnell, "Prescription Drugs and Medicare Reform," National Center for Policy Analysis *Brief Analysis*, no. 314, March 16, 2000. Reprinted with permission.

S hould the elderly have insurance for prescription drugs? Almost everyone says "yes" and it's not hard to understand why. Drugs not only are increasingly important to health care, they may be about the best buy available in the medical marketplace. New drugs are the main reason medical science has made amazing progress in recent years against cancer and heart disease. They have converted AIDS from a death sentence into a chronic illness. A 1996 study by the National Bureau of Economic Research shows that every dollar spent on prescription drugs is associated with a decrease of four dollars in hospital expenses.

President Clinton and some on Capitol Hill [have proposed] a costly prescription drug benefit for the elderly that could create huge new burdens for taxpayers. Fortunately, there is a way to solve the problem without costing taxpayers a single dime.

## The Shortcomings of Medicare and Medigap

Despite its political popularity, Medicare violates almost all principles of sound insurance. It pays too many small bills the elderly could easily afford on their own, while leaving them exposed to thousands of dollars of potential out-of-pocket expenses, including the cost of their drugs. Each year about 360,000 Medicare beneficiaries spend more than $5,000 out-of-pocket.

To prevent financial devastation from medical expenses, about two-thirds of Medicare beneficiaries acquire supplemental insurance, either through a former employer or by direct purchase. Although some Medigap policies cover prescriptions, most do not, and among those that do, coverage is often incomplete. Ironically, the poorest seniors often have the best drug coverage because they qualify for Medicaid, the federal-state health program for the poor. Where prescription drug coverage is incomplete or nonexistent, doctors and patients may turn to more expensive therapies—for example, opting for surgery for heart disease instead of treating it with drugs— because insurance will pay the bills. Health economists estimate that seniors with both Medicare and Medigap spend about 30 percent more on health care than those with Medicare alone.

The elderly could have better health care coverage—including a prescription drug benefit—if they were allowed to combine their Medicare funds with the money they currently spend on private insurance and pay one premium into a comprehensive private plan. Medicare will spend about $5,800 on each beneficiary in 2000. Add to that about $1,600—the amount seniors are already paying for the most popular Medigap policy—and the combined sum should be enough to buy the same kinds of health insurance coverage the nonelderly now have, including prescription drug coverage. That's the conclusion of a study prepared for the National Center for Policy Analysis by Milliman & Robertson, Inc., the nation's leading actuarial firm on health benefits. . . . [According to the study:]

- With the money Medicare would have spent plus the cost of the most popular Medigap policy, plus another $150 a year, an average senior could get comprehensive coverage from a Health Maintenance Organization (HMO), comparable to the coverage nonelderly HMO members have.
- The senior would have to make small copayments to discourage abuse, say $10 for a doctor visit or a drug purchase, but he or she could expect to save about $500 a year in out-of-pocket costs while avoiding the potentially unlimited out-of-pocket expenses of the current system.
- Seniors who want more choices could enroll in a fee-for-service plan with a high deductible and a Medical Savings Account, usually for a lower premium than they currently pay for Medigap insurance; the out-of-pocket cost should average about $1,500 a year—far less than the unlimited exposure most seniors now face.
- On the average, seniors who choose a private fee-for-service plan over the current Medicare/Medigap arrangement would save more than $1,000 a year in out-of-pocket costs.

Congress thought it was allowing seniors to use their Medicare money to join private health plans when it passed Medicare+Choice in 1997. The program was supposed to give the elderly the full range of health insurance options currently available to nonseniors: HMOs, Medical Savings Accounts

(MSAs), fee-for-service plans, doctor-run plans, etc. However, the federal Health Care Financing Administration (HCFA), which regulates Medicare, is hostile to private insurance, hostile to competition and hostile to choice. As a consequence, the program is saddled with so many rules, regulations and constraints that seniors have few of the options originally promised. For example:

- Seniors currently have no access to private fee-for-service plans, MSA plans or doctor-run plans; the one option that has survived is the Medicare HMO.
- Although 16 percent of seniors shifted out of traditional Medicare and into HMOs, HCFA cut the reimbursement rates to HMOs [in 1999], forcing many insurers out of the program.
- This left almost half a million seniors, many of whom had drug coverage, scrambling to find another HMO or

## Another Way to Pay for Prescription Drugs

The most appealing private option [for Medicare reform] is probably medical savings accounts (MSAs). With an MSA, instead of all health funds going to an insurance company, only a modest portion is paid to an insurer for catastrophic insurance, which typically covers all bills over a high deductible like $3,000 per year. The rest of the funds would be paid into an individual account for each retiree or worker. The covered patient could then use the funds in the account to pay medical bills below the deductible amount. Moreover, a patient could use funds in his MSA for any medical services or treatments he needed. Whatever account funds the patient did not spend on health care could be withdrawn at the end of the year and used for any purpose, or saved for future use. . . .

The MSA funds can be used to pay for any health service or treatment the retiree chooses, from any doctor, hospital, or other health provider the retiree chooses. This includes health services and treatments not covered by Medicare. For example, in some years many retirees will not have to see a doctor much, but they may have high expenses for prescription drugs not covered by Medicare. With an MSA, the retiree could use the funds in the MSA to pay for the prescription drugs. MSA funds can also be used for any form of alternative, nontraditional medicine the patient may choose.

Peter J. Ferrara, *Cato Policy Analysis*, April 29, 1998.

return to traditional Medicare.

- Another 99 HMOs have announced their intent to leave the Medicare program [in 2000].

[In 1999] the National Bipartisan Commission on the Future of Medicare led by Senator John Breaux (D-Louisiana) and Representative Bill Thomas (R-California) proposed making it easier for seniors to enter a wide variety of private plans. Under their proposal, the government would subsidize the premiums of low-income seniors more generously than those of high-income seniors. More recently, Senators Breaux and Bill Frist (R-Tennessee) introduced a similar approach. Like the commission's proposal, the Breaux-Frist bill calls for Medicare to be restructured using the federal employees health plan as a model. Beneficiaries would be subsidized by the federal government (as they are today) and allowed to join one of a number of competing private plans. Depending on the plan they chose, seniors could pay as little as nothing or up to $45.50 a month extra for more comprehensive coverage. The bill also has subsidies for the neediest enrollees.

The biggest obstacle [was] the Clinton administration. The recommendation of the Medicare commission went nowhere when the president refused to endorse it and members of his administration actively tried to sabotage it. . . . [T]he president ha[d] also signaled his opposition to the bipartisan Breaux-Frist bill. Instead, President Clinton proposed a modest drug benefit under Medicare [in 1999] that would have done little to help those with really high prescription costs. The president [also] added money for catastrophic drug costs. However, the coverage is far from complete and the proposal does nothing to fundamentally solve the problems of Medicare.

We cannot solve the problem of prescription drug coverage for the elderly without addressing the structural problems of Medicare. Structural reform can be accomplished by building on the Medicare+Choice program that is already in place. The Milliman & Robertson study shows that seniors could use the combined funds from Medicare and supplemental insurance to enroll in comprehensive private health plans to obtain better insurance, including prescription drug coverage, with less out-of-pocket cost.

*"Horror stories involving nursing homes
have become almost commonplace."*

# The Aging Are Treated Poorly
# in Nursing Homes

Eric Bates

In the following viewpoint, Eric Bates asserts that nursing
homes provide shoddy—and frequently fatal—care to the
elderly. He details several fatal incidents in homes owned by
Beverly Enterprises, which controls more nursing-home
beds than any other firm of its kind. According to Bates,
Beverly Enterprises and other nursing home chains are
more interested in earning profits than ensuring that their
patients receive reliable care. Bates is a staff writer for the
*Independent*, a locally owned alternative weekly in Durham,
North Carolina.

As you read, consider the following questions:

1. According to the federal study cited by the author, what
   proportion of California nursing homes had been cited
   for fatal or life-threatening violations?
2. What led to the rise of privately run nursing homes, as
   explained by Bates?
3. According to Bates, what is the annual turnover in the
   nursing home industry?

Excerpted from Eric Bates, "The Shame of Our Nursing Homes: Millions for
Investors, Misery for the Elderly," *The Nation*, March 19, 1999. Reprinted with
permission.

The day before Kimberly Holdford left on a camping trip with her husband and twin girls in June of 1997, she stopped by a nursing home to visit her grandmother. It had been a month since Jewel Elizabeth Forester entered the Beverly Health and Rehabilitation Center in Jacksonville, Arkansas, to recover from a bout with the flu that had left her severely dehydrated. She hated the facility. Beverly aides seldom bathed her and often neglected to take her to the bathroom, leaving her caked in dried feces and sobbing in shame. Holdford didn't know what to do; Beverly was the only nearby nursing home with an available bed. "We're understaffed," she recalls an aide telling her. "We don't have enough people to do the job."

At 80, Forester remained feisty and sharp-witted, tackling crossword puzzles and reveling in the afternoon soaps. But on the day before the camping trip, Holdford found her groggy and disoriented. "What's wrong with my grandmother?" she asked the nursing staff. "She won't wake up." Assured that a doctor would be called, Holdford reluctantly left for the weekend.

But no one at Beverly called the doctor. The next day Forester was screaming in pain and moaning in her sleep. Aides tried to calm her down because she was disturbing other patients. On Monday a respiratory therapist found Forester nearly comatose. She was rushed to the hospital, where doctors found three times the maximum therapeutic level of a drug called digoxin in her system. The nursing home had administered an overdose of the drug, even though it had been warned that Forester had trouble tolerating the medication.

"What followed was nine days of the worst deathwatch you ever saw in your life," recalls Robert Holdford, Kimberly's husband. "She was screaming and moaning as her organs shut down from the overdose. She suffered an agonizing death because of Beverly."

## Nursing Home Horrors

Nor was Forester the only patient at the home to suffer from substandard care. With too small a staff to turn and feed them, some residents developed bone-deep wounds; one was hospitalized weighing only eighty-one pounds. [In September 1998] a 58-year-old man died after an untrained and unlicensed nurse punctured his stomach lining when she tried to reinsert a feeding tube.

Dan Springer, a vice president at Beverly, calls the facility "an aberration," but the company has acknowledged that things were seriously amiss. "We knew that we had some problems," a top executive told reporters after the home was finally shut down by the state. "It was horrible."

Such horror stories involving nursing homes have become almost commonplace. For three decades, federal and state investigations have repeatedly documented widespread understaffing, misuse of medication and restraints, even physical attacks on patients. Yet thousands of vulnerable citizens remain confined in depressing, debilitating—and often deadly—institutions like the one in Jacksonville. [In summer 1998], a federal study found that nearly one-third of all nursing homes in California had been cited for violations that caused death or life-threatening harm to patients. Federal officials charged with policing dangerous homes "generally took a lenient stance," William Scanlon, director of health financing and systems issues for the U.S. General Accounting Office (GAO), testified before a Senate panel in July 1998. "Homes can repeatedly harm residents without facing sanctions."

Federal officials are promising to subject nursing homes to closer scrutiny. . . . President Clinton ha[d] ordered a crackdown on repeat offenders, the Justice Department is investigating charges of fraud and abuse, and Congress is poised to reshape Medicare and other programs that pay for long-term care. Yet such efforts focus more on cutting costs than improving care; they fail to recognize that standards remain lax and reforms fall short because of the very nature of nursing homes. Facilities that care for nearly 2 million elderly and disabled residents form a lucrative private industry that profits directly from pain—while taxpayers foot the bill. Nursing homes ring up $87 billion of business each year, and more than 75 cents of every dollar comes from public funds through Medicaid and Medicare. The less of that money homes spend on care, the more they pocket for themselves and their shareholders. To ensure those profits, nursing homes are careful not to skimp when it comes to investing in politics: The industry gives millions in contributions to state and federal officials, ensuring weak public oversight.

## The Ills of Nursing Home Privatization

At a time when Republicans and Democrats alike are clamoring to let big business run everything from prisons to schools, nursing homes represent the nation's longest-running experiment in privatization—one that, after half a century, offers a graphic portrayal of what happens when private interests are permitted to monopolize public services. While the industry is currently struggling to adjust to new limits on Medicare spending, nursing homes still rely on a generous flow of public subsidies. Leading the for-profit field is Beverly Enterprises, which controls more nursing-home beds than any other firm in the nation. Founded in 1963 as privatization accelerated, the company now owns 561 homes like the one in Jacksonville, which is located just a few hours down the road from its corporate headquarters in Ft. Smith, Arkansas. Although Beverly posted a loss in 1998, it remains an industry giant. In 1997 the company enjoyed after-tax profits of $58.5 million on revenues of $3.2 billion.

The money did little to help elderly residents like Jewel Forester. "I trusted them not to let her come to harm," says Kimberly Holdford, looking at a photo of her grandmother. "Instead, this sweet little old woman who loved me all my life suffered a brutal death. Somebody has got to stop these big corporations from hurting our old people. They're supposed to be in the healthcare business, not the money-making business. All they care about is keeping profits up."

From colonial times, caring for the elderly poor has been a responsibility of government. At first, officials tried not only to pass the buck but to make a few as well. Until the 1820s villages and cities confronted with growing numbers of impoverished citizens routinely auctioned them off to families who provided squalid accommodations in return for grueling work. An observer at one Saturday-night auction at a village tavern noted that citizens "could speculate upon the bodily vigor and the probable capacity for hard labor of a half-witted boy, a forlorn-looking widow, or a halt and tottering old man." But as abuses—and profits—mounted, cities and counties began to operate their own poorhouses for the sick and aged. The expression "over the hill" comes from an 1871 ballad that depicts the plight of an old woman cast out by her children to live in a government-run workhouse.

© Konopacki/Rothco Cartoons. Used with permission.

As industrial mechanization eliminated jobs after World War I, the public began to protest overcrowding and illness in county poorhouses. Reformers often seemed less concerned about aiding the poor, however, than about keeping them away from the well-to-do. "Worthy people are thrown together with moral derelicts, with dope addicts, with prostitutes, bums, drunks—with whatever dregs of society happen to need the institution's shelter at the moment," the New York Commission on Old Age Security complained in a 1930 report. "People of culture and refinement," the commission noted, were forced to share services "with the crude and ignorant and feebleminded."

Spurred by scandals over conditions in public poorhouses, federal lawmakers decided to hand the elderly over to private industry. In 1935 Congress specifically framed the Social Security Act to prohibit cash payments to any "inmate of a public institution." Those over 65 received small monthly pensions, but none of the money could go to government-run homes for the aged. The massive transfer of tax dollars to private business fueled the creation of for-profit homes. Almost overnight, operators set up facilities to exploit pensioners. Sometimes little changed but the name. In Minnesota, private owners removed a large sign identifying the "Dodge County Poor Farm," replacing it with one reading "Fairview Rest Home." The federal government soon began making direct payments to private nursing homes and providing low-interest loans for construction, ensuring the fledgling industry a handsome profit. "So rapidly has the nursing home developed during the past 20 years," two observers noted in 1955, "that its history seems more like an eruption than an evolutionary development."

## A Big Business

The eruption became volcanic in 1965, when Congress created Medicaid to assist the elderly poor and Medicare to provide health insurance for the aged. The two programs provided a huge infusion of public money into private nursing homes, with few strings attached. Most states limited the number of homes, thus ensuring a supply of patients to fill the beds. They also reimbursed homes for all expenses, from mortgage and depreciation on the building to the staff and supplies inside—in essence, giving owners a blank check that virtually guaranteed them a healthy profit on their investment. Before long, global corporations like ITT rushed to cash in on the industry. With backing from Wall Street, the number of homes soared from 13,000 in 1967 to more than 23,000 in 1969.

"That was when nursing homes moved away from mom-and-pop operations to large, for-profit enterprises," says Charles Phillips, director of the Myers Research Institute in

Beachwood, Ohio. "They were more interested in real estate transactions than healthcare. They shuffled properties back and forth between subsidiaries, jacking up property costs to increase reimbursement. Our current long-term-care system is fundamentally a creature of government policy. Those real estate ventures became the source of corporate empires."

Today those empires represent a booming business. With the number of elderly citizens needing long-term care expected to double over the next two decades, Wall Street sees a steady stream of customers for nursing homes—with a guaranteed flow of cash consisting almost entirely of public funds. "We believe nursing homes are naturally well positioned to capitalize on this growing opportunity," the investment bank Hambrecht & Quist advised investors, predicting that corporate chains would boost profits by laying off staff members, cutting wages and doubling patient loads. With the help of large institutional investors like Goldman Sachs and Lazard Frères, nursing-home chains are also making shareholders happy by swallowing competitors at a record pace. In 1998 two of the largest chains in the country merged with two fellow giants, creating parent companies with annual revenues of about $3 billion each. Thanks to their big financial backers, seven chains now collect 20 cents of every dollar spent on nursing homes nationwide.

The oldest and largest chain is Beverly Enterprises. Founded by a California accountant at the outset of the federal bonanza, the company quickly earned him $10 million on his initial investment of $5,700. In the seventies, backed by the influential Arkansas brokerage house of Stephens, Inc., Beverly led the industry in a frenzied buying spree, adding nearly 1,000 nursing homes in less than a decade. "No other chain has been able to put together as successful an acquisition formula," reported a study by the Food and Allied Service Trades of the [American Federation of Labor-Congress of Industrial Organizations] (AFL-CIO).

For a time, Beverly found, bigger was better. For five years in the eighties the chain maintained an annual return on equity of 23 percent—the fifth-highest rate of any healthcare company nationwide. But unable to manage its far-flung network of nursing homes, Beverly lost $60 million in 1987 and began selling off facilities to avoid a hostile takeover. "We probably grew too fast," acknowledged David Banks, a former typewriter salesman and Stephens executive who now heads Beverly. . . .

## Lethal Cost-Cutting

Beverly certainly mirrors the industry in the way it cashes in on Medicaid and Medicare. To improve the bottom line, homes have funneled as much money as possible into property, administrative salaries and ancillary services like drugs and physical therapy, while cutting corners on patient care and staff wages. Many facilities have only one registered nurse on duty, relying on skeleton staffs of nurse's aides to provide almost all the hands-on care for dozens of patients. Most earn little more than the minimum wage and receive only seventy-five hours of training for difficult jobs that require them to monitor and feed patients and move frail and disabled residents with little assistance. Annual turnover industrywide is nearly 100 percent.

"They're short-staffing," says an aide at a Beverly home in Center Point, Alabama. "If you have twenty residents, it means you can't spend as much time with them as you should. You don't give residents the kind of care they deserve."

In nursing homes, skimping on labor costs can be lethal. In Minnesota, investigators found that at least eight residents at Beverly homes died after receiving inadequate care and supervision between 1986 and 1988. Myrtle Schneuer, 83, choked to death after a nurse's aide gave her bacon and toast, despite a doctor's order to feed her only soft food because she had difficulty swallowing. Lucy Gralish, 79, suffered for three hours after a heart attack before the home called a doctor. Joy Scales, 65, died of a skull fracture after an aide left her unattended on the toilet, contrary to her doctor's orders. "So much of this goes right back to the question of staffing and corner-cutting," James Varpness, the Minnesota ombudsman for older residents at the time, told reporters. "Why are people being left unattended on toilets so that they fall off and fracture their skull? It's because the nursing staff has too much to do and something else that needs to get done."

*"We continue to make solid progress in improving the quality of care and oversight in America's nursing homes."*

# The Quality of Nursing Homes Is Improving

Michael Hash

The quality of care in nursing homes is improving, Michael Hash asserts in the following viewpoint. According to Hash, this improvement is the result of the government's enforcement of tough nursing home regulations and a subsequent initiative that provided further protection to nursing home residents. Hash is the deputy administrator for the Health Care Financing Administration. This viewpoint is excerpted from testimony Hash gave in front of the Senate Special Committee on Aging in response to a report by the General Accounting Office on the quality of care in America's nursing homes.

As you read, consider the following questions:
1. What are some of the specific issues that the Health Care Financing Administration is addressing, according to Hash?
2. As stated by the author, who has the primary responsibility for conducting nursing home inspections?
3. What does Hash think is an essential element for the continued progress in America's nursing homes?

Excerpted from Michael Hash's testimony before the U.S. Senate Special Committee on Aging, November 4, 1999.

C hairman [Charles] Grassley, Senator [John] Breaux, distinguished Committee members, thank you for inviting me to discuss our efforts to improve oversight and quality of care for America's 1.6 million nursing home residents. I would also like to thank the General Accounting Office (GAO) for its continued involvement and evaluation, and for its recognition of our progress and commitment.

We have been aggressively working to improve protections for vulnerable nursing home residents since 1995, when the Clinton Administration began enforcing the toughest nursing home regulations ever. This and earlier GAO reports help to sharpen our focus in these efforts. We agree with the GAO that enhanced oversight of State surveyors is critical for improving the quality of care in our nation's 17,000 nursing homes. And we are already addressing many of the specific issues raised in this GAO report.

- We are working to increase consistency, cooperation, and communication among our regional offices.
- We continue to refine protocols for federal oversight of State surveyors.
- We have held training conferences and satellite broadcasts for federal surveyors.
- We are developing measurable and reportable performance standards for State survey agencies, including definitions of inadequate performance and a listing of sanctions and remedies available under current law, which we will complete within 90 days.
- And we will redirect the State Agency Quality Improvement Program to be a consistent national program directly tied to these measurable performance standards.

While we have much left to do, we are beginning to see evidence that our nursing home initiative is having an impact. The number of violations identified per survey increased from 4.8 in the year preceding the initiative to 5.5 in the year since it began. The number of violations with actual harm or immediate jeopardy to resident health and safety identified per survey increased from 0.65 to 0.73. And the number of facilities terminated for violation of health and safety standards increased from 39 to 45.

We have been greatly aided in our efforts to improve protections for nursing home residents by the assistance of this Committee, and particularly by your leadership, Chairman Grassley, in helping us secure needed funding. We know you appreciate the challenge of implementing the 30 distinct, often complicated, and interrelated provisions we are working to implement. The tasks require dozens of agencies and thousands of individuals across the country to literally and substantially change the way they conduct their business. We are committed to taking all these, and any additional, actions that will help build upon our efforts. By continuing to work with you, the GAO, States, advocates and providers, we will together put an end to the intolerable situations that have caused this most vulnerable population to needlessly suffer. . . .

Protecting nursing home residents is a priority for this Administration and our Agency. We are committed to working with States, which have the primary responsibility for conducting inspections and protecting resident safety. Through the Medicare and Medicaid programs, the federal government provides funding to the States to conduct on-site inspections of nursing homes participating in Medicare and Medicaid and to recommend sanctions against those homes that violate health and safety rules.

In 1995, the Clinton Administration began enforcing the nation's toughest-ever nursing home regulations. These regulations brought about measurable improvement, as documented in our 1998 Report to Congress. However, that report and investigations by the GAO made clear that more needed to be done. President Clinton therefore announced a major new initiative to increase protections for vulnerable nursing home residents and to crack down on problem providers.

## Nursing Home Initiative Progress

We have made substantial progress in implementing many facets of this initiative.

- We published new protocols for conducting nursing

home surveys which specifically address areas where there have been significant problems, including hydration, nutrition, and pressure sores. These protocols are vital to guiding and training State surveyors and will assure a new level of consistency of surveying among the States.

- We provided training and guidance to States on the President's nursing home initiative, including enforcement, use of quality indicators in the survey process, survey tasks in the areas of medication review, pressure sores, dehydration, weight loss, and abuse prevention.
- We required States to evaluate all complaints alleging actual harm within 10 days. In October 1999 we issued detailed guidance on how to evaluate and prioritize complaints. Key staff from each of our regional offices will be meeting with State survey agencies to discuss these guidelines and facilitate sharing of best practices in complaint management.
- We identified facilities in each State for more frequent inspection and intense monitoring, based on results of most recent annual inspections and any substantiated complaints during the previous two years. States have begun monitoring these facilities more frequently.
- We vigorously encouraged States to impose sanctions on facilities that do not comply with health and safety regulations.
- We urged States to impose especially close scrutiny and immediate sanctions for facilities that demonstrate "yo-yo" compliance by fixing problems temporarily, only to be cited again in subsequent surveys.
- We instructed States to stagger surveys and conduct a set amount on weekends, early mornings, and evenings.
- We required States to revisit facilities in person to confirm that violations have been corrected before lifting sanctions.
- We issued regulations that enable States to impose civil money penalties for each serious incident.
- We have been working with the Department of Justice to improve referral for potential prosecution of egregious cases in which residents have been harmed.

- And we are testing an abuse intervention campaign in 10 States, with posters and other printed messages in nursing homes to inform residents and families about the signs of abuse and how to report it.

We also are taking steps to protect residents in facilities that may be experiencing financial or other difficulties from any disruptions or dislocations. We have made clear that filing for Chapter 11 bankruptcy does not diminish a facility's responsibility to provide residents with high quality care and a good quality of life. We issued monitoring protocols designed to help State surveyors and ombudsmen uncover early warning signals that might indicate the possibility that a facility in financial difficulty will fail to continue providing quality care to residents. And we developed a management contingency plan spelling out responsibilities of State and federal governments so we can respond quickly and effectively if a facility's financial situation places resident health or safety at risk.

## Evidence of Improvement

According to a report to Congress, there is clear evidence that current regulations are improving the health and safety of nursing home residents. Specifically:

- the overuse of anti-psychotics is down from about 33 percent before nursing home reform was implemented to 16 percent now;
- use of antidepressant is up from 12.6 percent to 24.9 percent, a rate more commensurate with the estimated nursing home prevalence of depression;
- the inappropriate use of physical restraints is down, from about 38 percent to under 15 percent;
- the inappropriate use of indwelling urinary catheters is down nearly 30 percent; and
- the number of nursing home residents with hearing problems who receive hearing aids is up 30 percent.

Health Care Financing Administration, "Assuring the Quality of Nursing Home Care," July 21, 1998.

To improve consistency in how these efforts are implemented across the country, we have established a workgroup that includes key central and regional office staff. This work-group is promoting clear and consistent communication among all involved staff. And it is specifically addressing areas where inconsistencies have been identified. . . .

## States Must Be Held Accountable

We agree with the GAO's assessment of the parameters of our ability to ensure State survey agency accountability. Given these limits, the most critical factor for assuring State accountability is to establish definitive and measurable standards for the quality of surveys.

We have been working with State agencies to establish definitive, measurable, and reportable performance standards. We expect to complete them by the end of 1999 and to then use them as the basis for holding States accountable. For example, these standards will address:

- the timeliness of surveys;
- the timeliness of adherence to enforcement procedures;
- expenditure of funds; and
- adherence to survey policies and protocols.

There will be minimum criteria for each performance standard. We will provide standardized instructions for our regional office staff on how to evaluate whether a State is meeting these criteria. And we will include definitions of inadequate performance and a listing of sanctions and remedies available under current law.

Once these standards are in place and States fully understand how they are being held accountable, we will redirect our State Agency Quality Improvement Program so that it is consistent nationwide and tied directly to these measurable and reportable performance standards. We will work with States that fail to meet the standards, using the appropriate remedy or sanction to help them improve when necessary. We also will evaluate the effectiveness of currently available sanctions, and explore alternative options for rewarding or sanctioning States based on their performance according to these measurable and reportable performance standards.

We continue to make solid progress in improving the quality of care and oversight in America's nursing homes. We agree that consistency in this effort is essential, and we are committed to consistency among our regional offices, clear guidance, better data systems, and measurable performance standards nationwide.

*"It is morally unacceptable that the people that built this country—our senior citizens—should suffer hunger in a land of plenty."*

# Hunger Among the Aging Needs to Be Prevented

America's Second Harvest

America's Second Harvest is the nation's largest domestic hunger-relief organization. In the following viewpoint, America's Second Harvest asserts that many of America's senior citizens suffer from serious hunger. According to research cited by the organization, 1.9 million seniors have had to choose between purchasing food and purchasing medicine, while 1.1 million seniors skipped meals because there was no food in their homes. The authors suggest steps that can be taken in order to ensure that the elderly receive the proper nutrition.

As you read, consider the following questions:

1. According to the authors, what are some of the health problems that can be worsened by hunger?
2. What percentage of emergency food client households served by America's Second Harvest receives Social Security?
3. Why does America's Second Harvest believe the food stamp participation rate among eligible elderly households has decreased?

Reprinted, with permission, from "Hunger and the Elderly," in *Who's Hungry: Facts and Figures on Hunger*, a web publication of America's Second Harvest, found at www.secondharvest.org/whoshungry/hunger_elderly.html.

A s a nation, we have a special responsibility to vulnerable populations like children and the elderly. Older Americans have built the economy and national infrastructure from which we now benefit. Raised during the Great Depression, they went on to defend our freedom in the Second World War and won the cold war. America's older citizens have rightly been called the "greatest generation." It is morally unacceptable that the people that built this country— our senior citizens—should suffer hunger in a land of plenty, which they helped to create.

## The Extent of Hunger Among the Elderly

Approximately 33 million Americans (13% of the population) are 65 years or older. Nearly 20% of older Americans, one in five, live in poverty or near poverty. Seniors who experience hunger are at risk for serious health problems. Hunger increases their risk for stroke, exacerbates pre-existing ill health conditions, limits the efficacy of many prescription drugs, and may affect brain chemistry increasing the incidence of depression and isolation.

Approximately 16%, or 4 million, of the emergency food clients served by the America's Second Harvest network are elderly. Seniors, however, only account for 13% of the U.S. population.

Seniors make up 16.5% of all emergency food pantry clients, 17% of all soup kitchen clients, 4% of all emergency shelters clients, and 17.5% of the clients served by other non-congregate feeding programs such as Meals on Wheels. 14% of households served by the America's Second Harvest network include a person over the age of 60.

According to research conducted by the Urban Institute, 1.9 million seniors must choose between buying food and buying needed medicine. America's Second Harvest research shows that 28% of all clients (includes all age groups) had to choose between buying food and buying medicine or filling prescriptions. The choice between food and medicine is not one that any American should have to make.

Approximately 28% of all emergency food clients have missed meals in the past month. Additional research has estimated that 1.1 million seniors have skipped meals because there is no food in the house.

*Hunger 1997: The Faces & Facts* reveals that 26% of all emergency food client households served by America's Second Harvest receive Social Security. Twenty-five percent of households with elderly persons participate in Senior Meals programs and 8.7% participate in home delivered meals programs like Meals on Wheels.

## The Establishment of Government Food Programs

In his 1972 budget message, President Nixon noted that "a new commitment to the aging is long overdue," and two nutrition programs were added that year: centralized, or congregate, meal sites—now numbering about 16,000—where seniors could eat a hot lunch and socialize; and a delivery service to send a hot meal to the homebound elderly. . . .

The food programs were supposed to promote "better health" among the older population "through improved nutrition" and offer "older Americans an opportunity to live their remaining years in dignity." Nixon pledged that the federal commitment would "help make the last days of our older Americans their best days."

At the beginning, Nixon tried to make good on that promise. When the Office of Management and Budget thought the initial funding should be $40 million and Nixon's adviser on aging, Arthur Flemming, suggested $60 million, Nixon upped the amount to $100 million. Throughout the seventies the funding kept pace with need. After that, however, it did not. Adjusting for inflation, per capita appropriations for all Older Americans Act programs in 1995 should have been $39. Actual per capita funding was only $19. Although total annual spending for all services has gone from $200 million in 1973 to $865 million today, that money not only hasn't kept up with inflation but it also hasn't kept up with the number of people who need help.

Trudy Lieberman, *Nation*, March 30, 1998.

In 1988, an estimated one-fourth of eligible seniors with incomes below the federal poverty level participated in the food stamp program. In contrast, 62 percent of elderly respondents with incomes below the federal poverty level participated in congregate meal programs, such as charitable food programs supplemented by The Emergency Food

Assistance Program (TEFAP) commodities. According to a 1994 [United States Department of Agriculture] (USDA)–Economic Research Service report, TEFAP recipients tend be older than Food Stamp Program recipients are (FSP is the primary national food assistance program). According to USDA, 40% of TEFAP recipient households were headed by someone aged 60 or older, as compared to only 15% of FSP households. An estimated 2 million elderly individuals (at age 50), participate in the food stamp program (7.1% of all food stamp participants, 1993).

Elderly individuals, accounting for approximately 18% of the population (aged 60 or older), account for roughly 30% of US health expenditures. Research suggests that insufficient nutrient intake accounts for a disproportionate amount of health care costs among low-income elderly individuals, unrelated to the aging process. The elderly that live in households with incomes below 130% of the federal poverty level tend to have lower nutrient intakes than other elderly households, thus exacerbating health concerns. Low-income blacks, urbanities, and Southerners generally consumed less of important nutrients than other demographic categories of the elderly.

## Recommendations for Change

In order to increase nutritional intake of low-income elderly individuals, we recommended that nutrition education materials—geared toward elderly individuals—be created and distributed at congregate feeding sites for the elderly. In addition, local food banks could make dieticians and other nutrition educators available to senior homes, congregate feeding sites and senior centers for nutrition education.

One principal reason for the reduced food stamp participation rate among eligible elderly households is the relative complexity of food stamp application and interview processes, and the stigma sometimes attached to food stamps as welfare. Therefore, it is recommended that case workers or volunteers meet income eligible seniors at congregate feeding sites and assist them in the application process. In addition, promotional materials should be created, geared toward seniors, which helps them to see that food stamp participation is an entitlement for life's work, just as social security is viewed by many aged individuals.

Additionally we recommend that state and federal government provide supplemental funding to increase home-based meal programs to five days a week for home-bound elderly individuals. We also recommend using food banks and other community-based hunger relief organizations to create additional congregate feeding sites in cooperation with similar human service agencies.

*"Older people are much more likely to age well than to become decrepit and dependent."*

# The Elderly Are in Good Health

John W. Rowe and Robert L. Kahn

In the following viewpoint John W. Rowe and Robert L. Kahn refute the myth that the elderly are in poor health. They contend that the prevalence of many medical conditions, including strokes and emphysema, have declined over recent decades. In addition, the authors assert, life expectancy has increased and seniors are likely to live independent lives well into their seventies or eighties. Rowe, a professor of medicine at the Mount Sinai School of Medicine in New York City, and Kahn, a professor emeritus of psychology and public health at the University of Michigan at Ann Arbor, were two of the researchers in the MacArthur Foundation Research Network on Successful Aging.

As you read, consider the following questions:

1. What are the two ways to determine if a person is able to remain independent, according to the authors?
2. As explained by Rowe and Kahn, what is the more negative school of thought on the implications of increased life expectancy?
3. According to Rowe and Kahn, what are the implications of the optimistic view of aging?

A central question regarding the status of the elderly is, "Just who is this new breed of seniors?" Are we facing an increased number of very sick old people, or is the new elder population healthier and more robust?

## Changes and Reductions in Diseases

The first clue comes in the prevalence of diseases. Throughout the century there has been a shift in the patterns of sickness in the aging population. In the past, acute, infectious illness dominated. Today, chronic illnesses are far more prevalent. The most common ailments in today's elderly include the following: arthritis (which affects nearly half of all old people), hypertension and heart disease (which affect nearly a third), diabetes (11 percent), and disorders which influence communication such as hearing impairment (32 percent), cataracts (17 percent), and other forms of visual impairments including macular degeneration (9 percent). When you compare sixty-five- to seventy-four-year-old individuals in 1960 with those similarly aged in 1990, you find a dramatic reduction in the prevalence of three important precursors to chronic disease: high blood pressure, high cholesterol levels, and smoking. We also know that between 1982 and 1989, there were significant reductions in the prevalence of arthritis, arteriosclerosis (hardening of the arteries), dementia, hypertension, stroke and emphysema (chronic lung disease), as well as a dramatic decrease in the average number of diseases an older person has. And dental health has improved as well. The proportion of older individuals with dental disease so severe as to result in their having no teeth has dropped from 55 percent in 1957 to 34 percent in 1980, and is currently approaching 20 percent.

But what really matters is not the number or type of diseases one has, but how those problems impact on one's ability to function. For instance, if you are told that a white male is age seventy-five, your ability to predict his functional status is limited. Even if you are given details of his medical history, and learn he has a history of hypertension, diabetes, and has had a heart attack in the past, you still couldn't say whether he is sitting on the Supreme Court of the United States or in a nursing home!

## Maintaining Independence

There are two key ways to determine people's ability to remain independent. One is to assess their ability to manage their personal care. The personal care activities include basic functions, such as dressing, bathing, toileting, feeding oneself, transferring from bed to chair, and walking. The second category of activities is known as nonpersonal care. These are tasks such as preparing meals, shopping, paying bills, using the telephone, cleaning the house, writing, and reading. A person is disabled or dependent when he or she cannot perform some of these usual activities without assistance. When you look at sixty-five-year-old American men, who have a total life expectancy of fifteen more years, the picture is a surprisingly positive one: twelve years are likely to be spent fully independent. By age eighty-five, the picture is more bleak: nearly half of the future years are spent inactive or dependent.

Life expectancy for women is substantially greater than that for men. At age sixty-five, women have almost nineteen years to live—four more than men of the same age. And for women, almost fourteen of those will be active, and five years dependent.

It is important to recognize that this dependency is not purely a function of physical impairments but represents, particularly in advanced age, a mixture of physical and cognitive impairment. Even at age eighty-five, women have a life expectancy advantage of nearly one and a half years over men and are likely to spend about half of the rest of their lives independent.

## Two Views on Life Expectancy

There are two general schools of thought regarding the implications of increased life expectancy on the overall health status of the aging population. One holds that the same advances in medical technology will produce not only longer life, but also less disease and disability in old age. This optimistic theory predicts a reduction in the incidence of nonfatal disorders such as arthritis, dementia, hearing impairment, diabetes, hypertension, and the like. It is known as the "compression of morbidity" theory—in a nutshell, it envisions prolonged active life and delayed disability for older people. A contrasting theory maintains just the opposite: that our population will become both older and sicker.

The optimistic theory may be likened to the tale of the "one-horse shay" by Oliver Wendell Holmes. Some sixty-five to seventy years ago, when [Robert L. Kahn] was reluctantly attending the Fairbanks Elementary School in Detroit, students were required to memorize poetry. One of Robert's favorites was a long set of verses by Oliver Wendell Holmes entitled "The Deacon's Masterpiece or The Wonderful One-Horse Shay." (A shay was a two-wheeled buggy, usually fitted with a folding top. The word itself, shay, is a New England adaptation from the French *chaise*.)

## Life Expectancy at Birth, According to Race and Sex: United States, Selected Years 1900–97

[Data are based on the National Vital Statistics System]

| Specified age and year | All races | | | White | | | Black | | |
|---|---|---|---|---|---|---|---|---|---|
| | Both sexes | Male | Female | Both sexes | Male | Female | Both sexes | Male | Female |
| At birth | Remaining life expectancy in years | | | | | | | | |
| 1900 ......... | 47.3 | 46.3 | 48.3 | 47.6 | 46.6 | 48.7 | 33.0 | 32.5 | 33.5 |
| 1950 ......... | 68.2 | 65.6 | 71.1 | 69.1 | 66.5 | 72.2 | 60.7 | 58.9 | 62.7 |
| 1960 ......... | 69.7 | 66.6 | 73.1 | 70.6 | 67.4 | 74.1 | 63.2 | 60.7 | 65.9 |
| 1970 ......... | 70.8 | 67.1 | 74.7 | 71.7 | 68.0 | 75.6 | 64.1 | 60.0 | 68.3 |
| 1980 ......... | 73.7 | 70.0 | 77.4 | 74.4 | 70.7 | 78.1 | 68.1 | 63.8 | 72.5 |
| 1985 ......... | 74.7 | 71.1 | 78.2 | 75.3 | 71.8 | 78.7 | 69.3 | 65.0 | 73.4 |
| 1986 ......... | 74.7 | 71.2 | 78.2 | 75.4 | 71.9 | 78.8 | 69.1 | 64.8 | 73.4 |
| 1987 ......... | 74.9 | 71.4 | 78.3 | 75.6 | 72.1 | 78.9 | 69.1 | 64.7 | 73.4 |
| 1988 ......... | 74.9 | 71.4 | 78.3 | 75.6 | 72.2 | 78.9 | 68.9 | 64.4 | 73.2 |
| 1989 ......... | 75.1 | 71.7 | 78.5 | 75.9 | 72.5 | 79.2 | 68.8 | 64.3 | 73.3 |
| 1990 ......... | 75.4 | 71.8 | 78.8 | 76.1 | 72.7 | 79.4 | 69.1 | 64.5 | 73.6 |
| 1991 ......... | 75.5 | 72.0 | 78.9 | 76.3 | 72.9 | 79.6 | 69.3 | 64.6 | 73.8 |
| 1992 ......... | 75.8 | 72.3 | 79.1 | 76.5 | 73.2 | 79.8 | 69.6 | 65.0 | 73.9 |
| 1993 ......... | 75.5 | 72.2 | 78.8 | 76.3 | 73.1 | 79.5 | 69.2 | 64.6 | 73.7 |
| 1994 ......... | 75.7 | 72.4 | 79.0 | 76.5 | 73.3 | 79.6 | 69.5 | 64.9 | 73.9 |
| 1995 ......... | 75.8 | 72.5 | 78.9 | 76.5 | 73.4 | 79.6 | 69.6 | 65.2 | 73.9 |
| 1996 ......... | 76.1 | 73.1 | 79.1 | 76.8 | 73.9 | 79.7 | 70.2 | 66.1 | 74.2 |
| 1997 ......... | 76.5 | 73.6 | 79.4 | 77.1 | 74.3 | 79.9 | 71.1 | 67.2 | 74.7 |

National Center for Health Statistics, *Health, United States*, 1999.

The relevance of all this to gerontology becomes clear early in the poem. The deacon was exasperated with the tendency of horse-drawn carriages to wear out irregularly; one part or another would fail when the rest of the vehicle was still in prime condition. He promised to build a shay in which every part was equally strong and durable, so that it would not be subject to the usual breakdowns of one or another part. And he was marvelously successful. The shay showed no sign of aging whatsoever until the first day of its 101st year, when it suddenly, instantly, and mysteriously turned to dust. The poem concludes with a line that stays in memory after all the intervening years. It is the poet's challenge to those who find the story difficult to believe. Since every part of the shay was equally durable, collapse of all had to come at the same moment: "End of the wonderful one-hoss shay; logic is logic; that's all I say."

The second, more negative theory—in which older people become sicker and more dependent with increasing age—is losing favor. MacArthur Studies and other research show us that older people are much more likely to age well than to become decrepit and dependent. The fact is, relatively few elderly people live in nursing homes. Only 5.2 percent of older people reside in such institutions, a figure which declined significantly from the 6.3 percent found in a 1982 survey. Furthermore, most older Americans are free of disabilities. Of those aged sixty-five to seventy-four in 1994, a full 89 percent report no disability whatsoever. While the proportion of elderly who are fully functioning and robust declines with advancing age, between the age of seventy-five to eighty-four, 73 percent still report no disability, and even after age eighty-five, 40 percent of the population is fully functional.

Between 1982 and 1994, the proportion of the population over age sixty-five that reported any disability fell from 24.9 percent to 21.3 percent, a meaningful reduction. And another statistic really sends the message home: in the United States today there are 1.4 million fewer disabled older people than there would be had the status of the elderly not improved since 1982. Furthermore, many studies show that the reduction in disability among older people appears to be accelerating. This is true at all ages, even among those over age ninety-five.

And so, the optimistic vision of aging seems to hold true—and the fact that the elderly population is relatively healthy and independent bears on the future of social policies for older people. It has important implications for issues as broad as establishing the proper eligibility age for Social Security benefits, and projecting the likely future expenses of federal health care programs including Medicare and Medicaid. Furthermore, beyond social policy implications, the greater our understanding of disability trends, the greater, in turn, will be our insights into the degree of biological change in our aging population. Disability in older people results from three key factors: 1) the impact of disease, or more commonly, many diseases at once; 2) lifestyle factors, such as exercise and diet, which directly influence physical fitness and risk of disease; and 3) the biological changes that occur with advancing age—formally known as senescence. It is not clear whether the reduction in the incidence of many chronic diseases—and the reduction in many risk factors for those diseases—is connected to a more general slowdown in the rate of physical aging. There is increasing evidence that the rate of physical aging is not, as we once believed, determined by genes alone. Lifestyle factors—which can be changed—have powerful influence as well. . . . It's a very empowering notion to keep in mind. We can, and should, take some responsibility for the way in which we grow older.

# Periodical Bibliography

The following articles have been selected to supplement the diverse views presented in this chapter. Addresses are provided for periodicals not indexed in the *Readers' Guide to Periodical Literature*, the *Alternative Press Index*, the *Social Sciences Index*, or the *Index to Legal Periodicals and Books*.

| | |
|---|---|
| *American Enterprise* | Special section on "Escaping the Medicare Crisis," July/August 1999. Available from 1150 17th St. NW, Washington, DC 20036. |
| Phil Benjamin | "Health Today," *Political Affairs*, June 2000. |
| John Buell | "Prescription Blackmail," *Humanist*, September/October 1999. |
| Robert N. Butler | "Living Longer, Contributing Longer," *Journal of the American Medical Association*, October 22, 1997. Available from PO Box 10945, Chicago, IL 60610. |
| Marilyn Chase | "Too Often, the Elderly Don't Get the Drugs or Care They Need," *Wall Street Journal*, September 24, 1999. |
| Mary H. Cooper | "Caring for the Elderly," *CQ Researcher*, February 20, 1998. Available from 1414 22nd St. NW, Washington, DC 20037. |
| *Health Affairs* | Special issue: "Future of Medicare," January/February 1999. Available from 7500 Old Georgetown Rd., Suite 600, Bethesda, MD 20814-6133. |
| Rosalie A. Kane | "Desperately Seeking Standards," *Aging Today*, July/August 1998. Available from 833 Market Street, Suite 511, San Francisco, CA 94103-1824. |
| Lucette Lagnado | "Drug Costs Can Leave Elderly a Grim Choice: Pills or Other Needs," *Wall Street Journal*, November 17, 1998. |
| Trudy Lieberman | "Hunger in America," *The Nation*, March 30, 1998. |
| *Newsweek* | "The Real Drug War," May 8, 2000. |
| Janet O'Keeffe and Jo Ann Lamphere | "Saving Medicare," *Issues in Science and Technology*, Summer 1998. |
| Virginia Postrel | "Dangerous Remedy," *Reason*, October 1999. |
| Sheryl Gay Stolberg | "Study Finds Pain of Oldest Is Ignored in Nursing Homes," *New York Times*, June 17, 1998. |
| Laura D'Andrea Tyson | "Healing Medicare," *American Prospect*, February 14, 2000. |

# For Further Discussion

## Chapter 1

1. After reading the viewpoints in this chapter, do you think that aging is a positive or negative experience? Explain your answer.

2. As a judge, Richard A. Posner approaches the question of age discrimination toward older workers from a legal standpoint. In contrast, Ursula Adler Falk and Gerhard Falk consider the issue from the perspective of a gerontologist and sociologist. How do you think their respective careers affect their arguments? Which argument do you find more convincing? Explain your answers.

## Chapter 2

1. Based on the viewpoints in this chapter, do you think that the aging population helps or hinders the American economy? Explain your answer.

2. Unlike the other authors in this chapter, Peter G. Peterson focuses on aging as a global issue, in particular how the world's economy will suffer as the elderly population grows. Do you agree with his suggestions for solving the problem, or do you think that his solutions are not applicable to all developed nations? Explain your answer.

3. Richard A. Lee asserts that the elderly will need increased help from outside services, provided by either the government or private companies. Virginia Stem Owens writes that aging adults are likely to turn to their children for assistance. Who do you think offers a more accurate reflection of elderly dependence and why?

## Chapter 3

1. After reading the viewpoints in this chapter, do you think that Social Security should be reformed? If so, what reforms should be implemented? Explain your answers.

2. Mark Weisbrot and Robert Kuttner contend that Social Security needs to be maintained because it is a program that seeks to ensure the well-being of all Americans. Do you think that Social Security is universally beneficial or that it helps some segments of the population at the expense of others? Explain your answers, drawing from the viewpoints and any other relevant material.

3. Darcy Ann Olsen asserts that women will be more financially secure during their retirement if Social Security is replaced by private accounts. The National Organization for Women dis-

agrees, contending that privatization is dangerous because it cannot ensure a steady income. Whose argument do you find more convincing, and why?

## Chapter 4

1. According to Sandra Mahkorn, the rules and regulations imposed by Medicare can seriously harm the health of seniors. Do you find her argument convincing? Why or why not?

2. Do you agree with Gail Shearer's contention that the cost-control mechanisms used in the private marketplace might not work with Medicare? Explain your answer.

3. Eric Bates details several incidents of negligent care in nursing homes. Do you think that the efforts made by the government to improve the quality of nursing homes, as detailed by Michael Hash, will be sufficient? Why or why not? What other steps do you think should be taken to protect nursing home patients?

# Organizations to Contact

The editors have compiled the following list of organizations concerned with issues debated in this book. The descriptions are derived from materials provided by the organizations. All have publications or information available for interested readers. The list was compiled on the date of publication of the present volume; the information provided here may change. Be aware that many organizations take several weeks or longer to respond to inquiries, so allow as much time as possible.

**AARP**
601 E St. NW, Washington, DC 20049
(800) 424-3410
e-mail: member@aarp.org • website: www.aarp.org

AARP, formerly known as the American Association of Retired Persons, is a nonpartisan association that seeks to improve the aging experience for all Americans. It is committed to the preservation of Social Security and Medicare. AARP publishes the magazine *Modern Maturity* and the newsletter *AARP Bulletin*. Issue statements and congressional testimony can be found at the website.

**Administration On Aging (AOA)**
330 Independence Ave. SW, Washington, DC 20201
(202) 619-7501 • fax: (202) 260-1012
e-mail: aoainfo@aoa.gov • website: www.aoa.dhhs.gov

The AOA works with a number of organizations, senior centers, and local service providers to help older people remain independent. It also works to protect the rights of the elderly, prevent crime and violence against older persons, and investigate health care fraud. AOA's publications include fact sheets on issues such as age discrimination, elder abuse, and Alzheimer's disease. Additional publications are available through AOA's National Aging Information Center.

**The Alzheimer's Association**
919 North Michigan Ave., Suite 1100, Chicago, Illinois 60611-1676
(800) 272-3900 • fax: (312) 335-1110
e-mail: info@alz.org • website: www.alz.org

The Alzheimer's Association is committed to finding a cure for Alzheimer's and helping those affected by the disease. The association funds research into the causes and treatments of Alzheimer's disease and provides education and support for people diagnosed with the condition, their families, and caregivers. Position statements and factsheets are available at its website.

## American Geriatrics Society
350 Fifth Ave., Suite 801, New York, NY 10118
(212) 308-1414 • fax: (212) 832-8646
e-mail: info@americangeriatrics.org • website:
www.americangeriatrics.org

The American Geriatrics Society (AGS) is a professional organization of health care providers that aims to improve the health and well-being of all older adults. AGS helps shape attitudes, policies, and practices regarding health care for older people. The society's publications include the book *The American Geriatrics Society's Complete Guide to Aging and Health*, the magazines *Journal of the American Geriatrics Society* and *Annals of Long-Term Care: Clinical Care and Aging*, and *The AGS Newsletter*.

## American Health Care Association (AHCA)
1201 L St. NW, Washington, DC 20005
(202) 842-4444 • fax: (202) 842-3860
website: www.ahca.org

AHCA is a federation of state associations of long-term health care facilities. It promotes standards for professionals in long-term health care delivery and quality care for patients and residents in a safe environment. AHCA publishes the monthly magazine *Provider* and the monthly newsletter *AHCA Notes*.

## American Society on Aging
833 Market St., Suite 511, San Francisco, CA 94103-1824
(415) 974-9600 • fax: (415) 974-0300
e-mail: info@asaging.org • website: www.asaging.org

The American Society on Aging is an organization of health care and social service professionals, researchers, educators, businesspersons, senior citizens, and policymakers that is concerned with all aspects of aging and works to enhance the well-being of older individuals. Its publications include the bimonthly newspaper *Aging Today* and the quarterly journal *Generations*.

## America's Second Harvest
116 S. Michigan Ave., Suite 4, Chicago, IL 60603
(800) 771-2303
website: www.secondharvest.org

America's Second Harvest is the nation's largest domestic hunger relief organization. It annually distributes food to 26 million

Americans, including the elderly, through a network of over two hundred food banks and food-rescue programs. America's Second Harvest also publishes *Update* magazine.

## Cato Institute

1000 Massachusetts Ave. NW, Washington, DC 20001-5403
(202) 842-0200 • fax: (202) 842-3490
e-mail: cato@cato.org • website: www.cato.org

The Cato Institute is a libertarian public policy research foundation dedicated to limiting the control of government and protecting individual liberties. Its Project on Social Security seeks to develop a viable plan for privatizing the Social Security system. In addition to the project, the institute provides books, articles, and studies about Social Security at its website, as well as articles and studies that support reforming Medicare. The Cato Institute publishes the magazines *Regulation* and *Cato Journal*.

## Gray Panthers

733 15th St., NW, Suite 437, Washington, DC 20005
(800) 280-5362 • fax: (202) 737-1160
e-mail: info@graypanthers.org • website: www.graypanthers.org

Gray Panthers is an intergenerational advocacy organization that works for social and economic justice. It focuses on issues such as universal health care, the preservation of Social Security, economic justice, and ageism. The Gray Panthers publish the bimonthly newsletter *Network* and the bimonthly publication *Points for Prowling*.

## International Federation on Ageing

425 Viger Ave. West, Suite 520, Montréal, Québec H2Z 1X2 Canada
(514) 396-3358 • fax: (514) 396-3378
e-mail: ifa@citenet.net • website: www.ifa-fiv.org

The International Federation on Ageing (IFA) is a private non-profit organization that brings together over 150 associations that represent or serve older persons in 54 nations. IFA is committed to ensuring the dignity and empowerment of older persons. It publishes the quarterly journal, *Ageing International*, and a monthly newsletter for its members, *Intercom*.

**Medicare Rights Center**
1460 Broadway, 11th Floor, New York, NY 10036
(212) 869-3850 • fax: (212) 869-3532
e-mail: jzurada@medicarerights.org • website:
www.medicarerights.org

The Medicare Rights Center (MRC) is a national organization that helps ensure that older adults receive quality affordable health care. It publishes a wide variety of Medicare materials, including a series of self-help pamphlets on Medicare issues and numerous booklets on Medicare-related topics.

**National Association for Home Care**
228 Seventh St. SE, Washington, DC 20003
(202) 547-7424 • fax: (202) 547-3540
e-mail: pr@nahc.org • website: www.nahc.org

The National Association for Home Care (NAHC) believes that Americans should receive health care and social services in their own homes. It represents home care agencies, hospices, and home care aide organizations. NAHC publishes the quarterly newspaper *Homecare News* and the monthly magazine *Caring*.

**National Citizens' Coalition for Nursing Home Reform (NCCNHR)**
1424 Sixteenth St. NW, Suite 202, Washington, DC 20036-2211
(202) 332-2275 • fax: (202) 332-2949
e-mail: nccnhr@nccnhr.org • website: www.nccnhr.org

The National Citizens' Coalition for Nursing Home Reform (NCCNHR) provides information and leadership on federal and state regulatory and legislative policy development and strategies to improve nursing home care and life for residents. Publications include the book *Nursing Homes: Getting Good Care There*, NCC-NHR's newsletter *Quality Care Advocate*, and fact sheets on issues such as abuse and neglect, restraints use, and how to choose a nursing home.

**National Council of Senior Citizens**
8403 Colesville Rd., Suite 1200, Silver Spring, MD 20910-3314
(301) 578-8800 • fax: (301) 578-8999
e-mail: communications@ncscinc.org • website: www.ncscinc.org

The National Council of Senior Citizens (NCSC) works to improve the lives of the elderly and people of all ages. It fights to protect Medicare, Medicaid, and Social Security and provides housing and jobs for the low-income elderly. Its bimonthly magazine, *Seniority*, is a bimonthly magazine focusing on issues and events that concern older Americans, while *The Senior Advocate* is NCSC's bi-monthly grassroots advocacy newsletter.

### National Council on the Aging (NCOA)
409 Third St. SW, Washington, DC 20024
(202) 479-1200 • fax: (202) 479-0735
e-mail: info@ncoa.org • website: www.ncoa.org

The NCOA is an association of organizations and professionals dedicated to promoting the dignity, self-determination, well-being, and contributions of older persons. It advocates business practices, societal attitudes, and public polices that promote vital aging. NCOA's quarterly magazine, *Journal of the National Council on the Aging*, provides tools and insights for community service organizations.

### National Institute on Aging (NIA)
Building 31, Room 5C27, 31 Center Dr., MSC 2292, Bethesda, MD 20892
(301) 496-1752
website: www.nih.gov/nia

The NIA, one of the twenty-five institutes and centers of the National Institutes of Health, spearheads a scientific effort to understand the nature of aging and to extend the healthy, active years of life. Its mission is to improve the health and well-being of older Americans through research. Publications available through the NIA include fact sheets, booklets, and *Connections* newsletter.

### The Seniors Coalition
9001 Braddock Rd., Suite 200, Springfield, VA 22151
(703) 239-1960 • fax: (703) 239-1985
e-mail: tsc@senior.org • website: www.senior.org

The Seniors Coalition, which positions itself as an alternative to the AARP, is a nonpartisan education and issue advocacy organization that represents the concerns of America's senior citizens. Its goals include protecting the Social Security Trust Fund and saving Medicare from bankruptcy. The coalition publishes *The Advocate* magazine.

# Bibliography of Books

Henry J. Aaron and Robert D. Reischauer — *Countdown to Reform: The Great Social Security Debate*. New York: Century Foundation Press, 2001.

Claude Amarnick — *Don't Put Me in a Nursing Home*. Deerfield Beach, FL: Garrett, 1996.

Dean Baker and Mark Weisbrot — *Social Security: The Phony Crisis*. Chicago: University of Chicago Press, 1999.

Margret M. Baltes — *The Many Faces of Dependency in Old Age*. Cambridge, England: Cambridge University Press, 1996.

Sam Beard — *Restoring Hope in America: The Social Security Solution*. San Francisco: Institute for Contemporary Studies, 1996.

Robert H. Binstock, Leighton E. Cluff, and Otto von Mering, eds. — *The Future of Long-Term Care: Social and Policy Issues*. Baltimore: Johns Hopkins University Press, 1996.

Robert H. Binstock and Linda K. George, eds. — *Handbook of Aging and the Social Sciences*. San Diego: Academic Press, 1996.

Jimmy Carter — *The Virtues of Aging*. New York: Ballantine, 1998.

Marshall N. Carter and William G. Shipman — *Promises to Keep: Saving Social Security's Dream*. Washington, DC: Regnery, 1996.

Martin Cetron and Owen Davies — *Cheating Death: The Promise and the Future Impact of Trying to Live Forever*. New York: St. Martin's Press, 1998.

William C. Cockerham — *This Aging Society*. Upper Saddle River, NJ: Prentice-Hall, 1997.

Peter A. Diamond, David C. Lindeman, and Howard Young, eds. — *Social Security: What Role for the Future?* Washington, DC: National Academy of Social Insurance, 1996.

Ursula Adler Falk and Gerhard Falk — *Ageism, the Aged and Aging in America: On Being Old in an Alienated Society*. Springfield, IL: Charles C. Thomas, 1997.

Peter J. Ferrara and Michael Tanner — *A New Deal for Social Security*. Washington, DC: Cato Institute, 1998.

Arthur D. Fisk and Wendy A. Rogers, eds. — *Handbook of Human Factors and the Older Adult*. San Diego: Academic Press, 1997.

Muriel R. Gillick — *Lifelines: Living Longer, Growing Frail, Taking Heart*. New York: W.W. Norton, 2000.

| Margaret Morganroth Gullette | *Declining to Decline: Cultural Combat and the Politics of the Midlife*. Charlottesville: University Press of Virginia, 1997. |
| Charles B. Inlander and Michael A. Donio | *Medicare Made Easy*. Allentown, PA: People's Medical Society, 1999. |
| Donald H. Kausler and Barry C. Kausler | *The Graying of America: An Encyclopedia of Aging, Health, Mind, and Behavior*. Urbana: University of Illinois Press, 2001. |
| Eric R. Kingson and James H. Schulz, eds. | *Social Security in the Twenty-First Century*. New York: Oxford University Press, 1997. |
| Thelma J. Lofquist | *Frail Elders and the Wounded Caregiver*. Portland, OR: Binford and Mort, 2001. |
| Joseph L. Matthews | *Social Security, Medicare, and Pensions*. Berkeley, CA: Nolo, 1999. |
| E.J. Myers | *Let's Get Rid of Social Security: How Americans Can Take Charge of Their Own Future*. Amherst, NY: Prometheus Books, 1996. |
| Evelyn M. O'Reilly | *Decoding the Cultural Stereotypes About Aging: New Perspectives on Aging Talk and Aging Issues*. New York: Garland, 1997. |
| S. Jay Olshansky and Bruce A. Carnes | *The Quest for Immortality: Science at the Frontiers of Aging*. New York: W.W. Norton, 2001. |
| Fred C. Pampel | *Aging, Social Inequality, and Public Policy*. Thousand Oaks, CA: Pine Forge Press, 1998. |
| Peter G. Peterson | *Gray Dawn: How the Coming Age Wave Will Transform America—And the World*. New York: Times Books, 1999. |
| Peter G. Peterson | *Will America Grow Up Before It Grows Old?: How the Coming Social Security Crisis Threatens You, Your Family, and Your Country*. New York: Random House, 1996. |
| John W. Rowe and Robert L. Kahn | *Successful Aging*. New York: Pantheon Books, 1998. |
| Sylvester J. Schieber and John B. Shoven | *The Real Deal: The History and Future of Social Security*. New Haven, CT: Yale University Press, 1999. |
| Ken Skala | *American Guidance for Seniors—And Their Caregivers*. Falls Church, VA: K. Skala, 1996. |
| Max J. Skidmore | *Social Security and Its Enemies: The Case for America's Most Efficient Insurance Program*. Boulder, CO: Westview Press, 1999. |

Richard D. Thau and
Jay S. Heflin, eds.
*Generations Apart: Xers vs. Boomers vs. the Elderly*. Amherst, NY: Prometheus Books, 1997.

Dale Van Atta
*Trust Betrayed: Inside the AARP*. Washington, DC: Regnery, 1998.

James W. Walters, ed.
*Choosing Who's to Live: Ethics and Aging*. Urbana: University of Illinois Press, 1996.

David A. Wise, ed.
*Facing the Age Wave*. Stanford, CA: Hoover Institution Press, Stanford University, 1997.

# Index